GO

PUBLISH

YOURSELF!

Katie Salidas

Katie Salidas

Go Publish Yourself!

Copyright © 2012 by Katie Salidas

Go Publish Yourself!
ISBN 978-0-9851277-0-1
First Edition - 2012
Format: Softcover
Cover Art: Willsin Rowe
Editing: Sharazade
Interior Formatting: Katie Salidas

Published by:
Rising Sign Books, LLC.
4600 E. Sunset Rd #279
Henderson Nv 89014

Praise for Go Publish Yourself!

"I learned from start to finish the easy steps from getting a cover artist and editor, to publishing on major sites like Amazon, to marketing and self-promoting, and so much more! Without this book I could have never done it on my own. This is a must-have book loaded with tips, tricks, and advice. I'm proud to say that thanks to Go Publish Yourself!, my book is up on Amazon and not collecting dust anymore!"

Chrissy Peebles
Author – Agartha's Castaways

"Written in clear, simple language, this guide takes you through all the steps to self-publishing for independent authors, for both ebooks and print books. The author is self-published herself, and is very open and honest about what worked and didn't work for her. There is so much in here--the various places you can publish, how-to's for formatting, do's and don'ts for marketing and promotion, what's worth paying for and what you can do yourself. Lots of addresses and links, for everything from the US Copyright Office to publishing software to recommended cover designers."

1001 Nights Press' books are a direct result of having used this guide.

What's in the Book?

Think of this book as a handy dandy guide to help you get through the major stumbling blocks on the route to becoming a self, or independent publisher.

I am an independent (indie) publisher. I've released seven titles to date with more on the way. Each of those titles was done DIY (Do It Yourself) style without the aid of author service companies. What items I could not handle on my own were contracted out to freelancers who specialized in their field: editing and cover design (I'll be providing some links for you later).

Why am I telling you all of this? It's not to brag, it's to show you that I know what I'm talking about. I've been there. I've stumbled through the steps and found, through experience, what works and what doesn't.

Go ahead and look me up by name. Check out the titles I've produced and the consumer ratings on those various books. I want you to feel safe that the knowledge I'm giving you is legitimate and has been tested in the market.

No single "How to" book will contain every minute detail involved in self-publishing. In fact, you could probably buy twenty books on self-publishing, and find that even after reading them all, you're still missing information. What this book will do, is give you the no-nonsense basic information and general steps to take to feel confident enough to publish your book in multiple formats.

Table of Contents

GO
PUBLISH
YOURSELF!

Deciding to Self-Publish

Self-publishing and indie publishing are interchangeable terms. Both mean that you, the author, take on all roles and responsibilities involved in the creation of your printed and bound (or epublished) book.

Self-publishing has come a long way in recent years. It used to be thrown around like a dirty word. Many thought of self-publishing as a refuge for those aspiring authors who couldn't get traditionally published. Self-publishing was a scarlet letter: a dirty little secret that you only told your friends and family. Literary agents publically cautioned aspiring authors to not tell them about self-published books because it would ruin the chances they'd consider their manuscript.

Today, however, self-publishing has taken on a new role. It's no longer the last resort of an author who has exhausted all traditional routes. Literary agents are even combing through self-published books available on Kindle or the Nook, searching for their next author to represent. I've known quite a few independent authors who have signed with agents and use them regularly for things like foreign rights and movie options. More still are signing with major publishers after finding success with their independently published books. These same authors had tried for years before to attract those publishers. If it weren't for their initiative and drive to self-publish, they would never have seen those deals.

In addition to the hope of landing a traditional contract, many authors are turning first to self-publishing for the freedom it allows them and the level of control it gives them in their work. And of course, self-publishing means a larger chunk of the royalties on each sale. That reason alone drives many authors to try self-publishing.

So, is self-publishing right for you?

Only you can answer that.

I'm not here to tell you what you should do. Each writer must take their own path.

But, chances are, if you're reading this, then you've already got a pretty good idea of what you want to do.

Great! Let's get started.

I'm going to be straightforward and honest with you in this book. I'll give you the good, the bad, and the ugly in a quick and dirty, no-nonsense manner. After reading this, you should feel confident in your decision and ready to take the various steps to getting your book out there.

Why are you Self-Publishing?

The first thing you need to consider, when looking at self-publishing, is what you want out of it. Why are you publishing, and what are your goals?

Are you doing this simply to hold your book printed and bound, in your hand? Are you looking to establish yourself as an indie author? Are you looking for fame and fortune? Is this a one-time book or a series you're working on? Are you expecting millions?

Let me break your heart for a minute. (Remember: I promised the good, the bad, and the ugly. I won't lie to you.)

Self-publishing is not the fast track to easy money!

I'm sure you've heard the stories about HP Mallory, Amanda Hocking, J. A. Konrath, and the list goes on. Please don't let the recent news about indie authors "selling millions" fool you. Just like with traditional publishing, the "millionaire authors" are more the exception than the rule. Self-publishing does not guarantee riches. For all of the authors you have heard about, there are thousands of others that you haven't.

Now that we've gotten that out of the way, don't let those facts discourage you. You can make a living wage from your writing, but you'll have to put in the effort. This is why you need to go into this with a clear head and know your goals.

It can take years to establish yourself in the market. For some, "overnight success" takes ten years. You have to be willing to accept that and do all you can to soldier through the rough patches.

Before you take any steps toward creating your book, sit down and have a real heart-to-heart about what you want and what your realistic goals are.

If you're doing this to have a few copies to share with friends and family (and that is just fine), then I'd suggest going the vanity publishing route via author service companies. Places like iUniverse or Trafford will take your manuscript (your completed story in a word-processed format) and perform all the tasks necessary (editing, interior layout, cover art, etc.) to turn it into a printed and bound book. They'll give you exactly what you're looking for: a bright, shiny new book with your name on it!

QUICK & DIRTY TIP!

Service-based publishing companies make their money by doing it all for you. They will charge you for that easy book creation, and it won't be cheap. This is not the option to take if you want to make money from your work.

If you're in this to truly become an indie author, then you need to treat your book like a business venture.

You might want to consider setting yourself up as a DBA (Doing Business As) or an LLC (Limited Liability Company). Creating a separate entity for your publishing venture will offer you some additional options when it comes to printing. Some companies will not work with individual authors (Lightning Source, a major printer and distributor, for example). That is not to say that you have to create a company for your publishing venture; it is just an option that can make things a little easier. We will not be going into the details of creating an LLC or DBA; that is beyond the scope of this book. I do, however, strongly suggest that you look into this option. Pick up a book or two at your local library.

In essence, that's exactly what self-publishing is: a business venture. Your business is the creation of a product: your book(s). You're putting this product out into the market with the hopes of making money from it. You have to take all the financial risk in this venture with no guarantee of a return on your investment.

Self-publishing is not for everyone. You need to go into this with a clear head and the willingness to give it your all. If you can't do this, then you might want to reevaluate your goals. If you can do this, however, then you'll reap the benefits of all that hard work and create a product that can eventually earn you a profit.

Common Misconceptions about Self-publishing

Because self-publishing is still in the early stages of being recognized as a viable platform, there are still old misconceptions being thrown around. These are used to scare potential indie authors away from taking that leap into the market.

"You'll be lucky to sell 200 copies."

This was the first thing I was told when I decided to self-publish my first novel *Immortalis Carpe Noctem*. It scared me, as it was meant to. But after talking with other indie authors and looking at the sales rankings on Kindle and other online platforms, I realized that this was completely untrue. A well-plotted book that has been edited and has good cover art sells just as well as its traditionally published counterpart. In fact, *Immortalis Carpe Noctem* sold more than 200 copies (print and ebooks combined) within the first couple of months of publication. It sold more than ten-thousand copies in its first year, and the number rises every day.

As you can see, the quote above is wrong; however, there is a seed of information there that you should take from it. No book will sell without help. I didn't just place my book online and hope for sales. To start, I made sure the book was edited, two times, and then gave it a beautiful cover. Those two items are essential to the potential success of your book. Beyond that, to get *Immortalis Carpe Noctem* to move, I had to market it. Getting the book online to vendors is just part of the process. Do not think that hitting "submit" will be the final step in your publishing journey. That is only the starting point. We'll discuss marketing in later chapters.

"Self-publishing will ruin your chances of ever being traditionally published."

Another thing I was told when I decided to self-publish was that it would ruin my chances to ever be traditionally published. That idea is the old style of thinking. Many authors today whose books show great promise are being targeted by literary agents. Instead of the author querying an agent and then waiting months for a response, the agents—after seeing excellent sales—are contacting authors directly to offer representation for things such as print rights, foreign rights, and movie options. In essence, the indie market is becoming a sort of slush pile for these agents.

Now, as with all things, there still is some truth to take from this quote. Only the books that are selling well will attract literary agents. If you are dabbling with both self-publishing and still considering the traditional route, I'd recommend not bragging about your "publishing achievements" if your book has not shown continuous positive sales. Remember that it takes time to build an audience, and you cannot expect overnight success. If you are straddling the fence between these two methods of publishing, keep them separate until you have something that is really worth bragging about.

"Only friends and family will buy your books."

This quote makes me laugh every time I hear it. In actuality, your friends and family will expect you to give them the book you publish for free. As they see it, they helped and supported you, so the least you can do is give them a free book.

And that's just fine. Give them a free copy. You're not marketing to them. As an indie author, you want strangers to buy your book. Focus all of your marketing efforts on building a platform and getting to know new readers. Those are the people you want to connect with and turn into fans.

The Business of Self-Publishing

Though self-publishing suggests DIY (Do It Yourself), most of us are not able to do all of the things required to create a book. That's okay. In most cases you won't be able to do it all, and for some things, like editing, you shouldn't. You'll probably have to contract out for things like cover art, editing, layout (in some cases), and so on.

All the money you spend toward the production of your book is a gamble. Remember this. There is no guarantee your book will sell, no matter how much money you throw into it. I'm not trying to suggest that you won't make any money on your book, but you do need to be very realistic in your goals and keep a very level head where costs are concerned. You should never go into these separate contract works with a blank check mentality. Spending $500 on a book cover might not be the smartest decision, even if the artwork is spectacular. That $500 will have to be made up in sales (along with all of your other production costs) before your book can begin to make you money. All costs need to be weighed out carefully. You should always be on the lookout for "the best bang for your buck."

Before you take any steps in the production of your book, sit down and create a budget. In the next section I will list the various places you will need to spend your book production money. Use that as a guide to help you create your budget and set limits on how much money to invest in your book. Make sure you have marketing money in your budget.

Basic Costs of Self-Publishing

Your product (your book) is a direct reflection of the work you've put into it and the money you've put into producing it. While it is important for you to produce the best-looking book you can, you still have to remain cost-conscious. You have to find the balance between quality and affordability.

I've seen many people with the "You can't put a price on art or quality" thought process. I'm not saying they're wrong. But this often leads authors to adopt a "blank check" mentality. They become willing to pay whatever it takes to have the best, and their budget goes out the window. When this happens, it could set your book's break-even point so high it might take years to hit.

QUICK & DIRTY TIP!

Authors often forget to factor the post-production money into their total costs. There are plenty of ways to bleed cash when it comes to marketing. Setting a spending limit before-hand will help you to avoid sinking more money than you wanted into the cost of the book.

Any good business person is going to do their research and find the most cost-effective way to do things before they invest. And so should every indie author. Don't overextend yourself by drowning your book in debt before it hits the market. Your book needs to be able to recoup its cost before it can make you any money.

Remember this: Make it your mantra when you're tempted to spend more than you had originally budgeted.

Now, let's take a quick look at some of the basic production costs.

Please note that this section gives you a general overview of the cost and why. We will delve deeper into each of these topics in their own sections later in this book.

1)   Write the book and get it critiqued: FREE

Critiquing Partner/Group: A person or a group of people who read and offer feedback and editing advice on some or all of an author's manuscript.

Before sending your manuscript to an editor, use a critique group or partner to help you polish your manuscript.

If there are no local critiquing groups in your area, check online writers' groups. There are plenty of them out there; just make sure that your work is protected when you post it. Look through the rules and FAQ's for the site and make sure your work is not searchable via sites like Google. You don't want your book all over the Internet before you publish it.

We will go into more detail about critiquing relationships in a later section.

2)   Professional Editing: $200 - $The sky is the limit!

Simple research will bring up hundreds of options where freelance editing is concerned. You could spend anywhere from $200 to $2,000 on this step alone.

High price does not always equal better quality work. My first editor charged me close to $1,000 to edit *Immortalis Carpe Noctem*. When it was done and published, the single biggest complaint I received was "poor editing." I spent a lot of time researching freelance editors and ended up finding one that did twice the job for less.

We'll discuss finding and evaluating editors in a later section.

3)   Printing and Distribution: $0 - $117 (Book setup for print only)

For most independent publishers, "printers" and "distributors" are terms used interchangeably. Unless you plan on going door-to-door with a stack of books, you want a printer who can also act as a distributor. This means you don't have to worry about warehousing and offset printing issues when trying to get your book onto bookstore shelves.

The printer you choose will have set fees for setting up your book. Make sure you know what those fees are before you decide to use them.

For example: Lightning Source charges $35 for setup of each file (book interior & book cover), plus a listing fee, and optional fees for proofs.

Createspace, another popular choice for independent publishers, has various plans for book setup and distribution for you to choose from.

No matter who you choose, you want to have your printer selected before you move on to further steps in the book process. The printer you work with will have very specific requirements for book formatting and layout that will affect the rest of your book production.

We will delve deeper into printing methods and the two top printer/distributors in later chapters.

4)   Book Layout: $0 - $400

This is the process by which you turn your word processed manuscript into a format that is ready to print. Also known as an "interior book block."

This can be done in Microsoft Word (or whatever word processor program you chose to use), but it's quite a frustrating process. The layout is how your book will look when printed: all of those fun little details like headers and footers, font, page breaks, page size, margins, etc.

You can hire out for this, or you can look for programs that help you do it yourself. We will look at this in-depth in later sections.

5) Book Cover Design: $50 - $The sky is the limit!

You can easily find artists willing to create a beautiful cover for you, and the rates will vary just as widely as for editing. If you've created your budget ahead of time, you will have a much better idea of what you can afford. Again, price does not always equal better workmanship. Sometimes it's just expensive to be expensive. I've seen beautiful covers made for $80, and equally beautiful covers made for $1,000. Only you can decide what is affordable for you, but keep your budget in check.

QUICK & DIRTY TIP!

Your designer will want to know some things before he or she makes your cover. I learned this the hard way.
- ✓ Know what your book dimensions will be before this step.
- ✓ Know the page count, know the trim size (the measurements of the book), softcover, hardcover, or ebook.
- ✓ Do your book layout first.

6) ISBNs: $10+ (Mostly for print but sometimes required for ebooks as well)

An ISBN (International Standard Book Number) is your publishing "social security number." It is a 13-digit string of numbers that identifies the book, the publisher, and what format it's in: ebook, softcover, hardcover, or audio.

A unique ISBN is required for each format of your book, so you'll have to purchase an ISBN for the various formats you plan on producing. If you're planning on releasing multiple books, the cost of your ISBN goes down significantly. Check the link here for the various pricing packages that are currently available. Also, ebook distributors like Smashwords and Pubit offer the option of using their ISBN for cheap ($10) or free.

http://www.isbn.org/standards/home/index.asp

7) PCN or LCCN: The cost of one print book + the postage to mail it

An LCCN (Library of Congress Catalog Number) and/or PCN (Pre-assigned Control Number) assigns a library cataloging number to your book. These numbers are only for print books and are only necessary if you want to get your print books into libraries.

http://pcn.loc.gov/pcn001.html

There is no charge for an LCCN or a PCN; however, you are obligated to send a complimentary copy of all books for which a LCCN or a PCN was provided immediately upon publication.

Library of Congress
US & Publisher Liaison Division
Cataloging in Publication Program
101 Independence Avenue, S.E.
Washington, D.C. 20540-4283

8) Copyright: $35

Copyright: The author's legal right to ownership of the work under federal copyright laws.

Just by writing it, your book is covered under copyright protection. However, without filing your registration, you'll find it very difficult to enforce.

Thankfully, you can easily file your copyright online! Yay!

http://www.copyright.gov/

Marketing Costs:
Don't Forget to Budget for This!

In the last section, I gave a rundown of basic costs for producing a book, but let's not forget marketing costs in your preliminary budget. Doing this ahead of time will help you avoid overspending. Remember that your book will only make money once it has hit the break-even point. All costs associated with production and marketing have to be covered before you make any money.

So, let's take a quick look at some of the things to consider for marketing your work and their potential associated cost. We will go into more detail later; this will just give you an overview.

1)   Website or Blog: $10 - $The sky is the limit

You need to have a presence on the Internet where people can find you and learn more about you and your work. There is no getting around this. We live in the digital age, and people are used to being able to type something (like your author name) into Google to find out whatever they want. And really, that's what you want too. You want people to have easy access and a place to find out the information you want to share with them. Aside from the obvious social networking sites like Facebook, Twitter, & Goodreads, you'll want a home of your own on the Web.

At the very minimum, you are looking at $10 to purchase a domain name (your personal Web address) that is registered to you. For instance, mine is:
http://www.katiesalidas.com.
If a potential reader wants to look me up, the best way for me to make it easy for them is to use my name as my website.

QUICK & DIRTY TIP!

A domain name does not mean you have a Website—just an address. You'll still need a place for that web address to point to. Many of the free blogging sites like Blogger or Word-Press allow you to use your personal domain name instead of their blog address. For a new author starting out, this is your most cost-effective way of creating a Web presence.

2) Book Reviews and Blog Tours: $100+

Book Blog Tour: A relatively new method of marketing an author's book via online blogs. An author and his/her book will be scheduled at a variety of blogs for interviews, book reviews, guest posts, and chapter excerpts. This avoids the author needing to physically travel around the country, yet still provides the opportunity to reach a wide audience.

The single best way to get the word out about your new book is to get it into the hands of people who read and review books publicly. This is where blog touring has taken off.

There are plenty of blog tour companies out there who will take your book and not only get it into the hands of other book reviewers, they'll also schedule those reviews up into a nice week-to-month tour through associated blogs and social networking sites.

This is a great service to look into; however, the cost can be high. Again, just like with all things I've mentioned, doing a little homework can mean the difference between spending $100 and spending $1,000.

You don't have to do a blog tour. There are free alternatives, but they will require a lot of work on your part. There are literally hundreds of bloggers out there who are willing to look at self-published books. You can hunt them down and request reviews by yourself too. It might take a little longer to get the reviews, but those reviews will cost you nothing more than the price of a book plus postage (in the case of print books) or free (in the case of ebooks).

QUICK & DIRTY TIP!

The single best resource I have found for locating book reviewers is this listing of over 400 sites willing to review indie authors. The list gets larger every day!

http://hampton-networks.com/category/indie-review-blogs/

Will *all* of these sites be right for your book? No. But many might be. If the list seems too daunting, they also have listing for blog tour companies. We will discuss those further in a later chapter.

3)   Bookmarks, Posters, Business cards, etc.: $Variable pricing, depending on the printer you choose.

SWAG (Stuff We All Get): A common term at conferences and tradeshows describing the freebies that are given away: bookmarks, posters, business cards, t-shirts, pens, etc. These are "freebies" you give away to help promote your book. While not essential, they are a handy tool that can showcase your book, tell people where to find you, and give them a reason to come back to your work in the future.

People like getting freebies. It helps to build a sense of goodwill with your potential new reader. In general, it's best to set aside at least a hundred dollars here to ensure you can create all of the goodies you want. We'll go more in-depth on this later.

4)   Paid Advertising: $10 - $The sky's the limit!

There are various places where you can pay to have your book listed. Some are "per click" advertising services, and some are flat fee. While it is not necessary for you to pay for any advertising for your books (there is no guarantee it will make them sell), there are a few you might consider looking at.

http://redadeptreviews.com/ - Banner ads and sidebar book ads as cheap as $10

http://www.kindleboards.com/ - Banner ads and Book of the Day ads $35-$195

http://kindlenationdaily.com/ - A high-traffic book promotion site with various ways to feature your work with equally variable prices.

http://www.projectwonderful.com/ - Bid on various advertisements

http://thefrugalereader.com/ - Various advertising packages

http://www.goodreads.com/advertisers - Pay Per Click

As I said before, these are things you might want to consider. We will go into more marketing detail in later chapters. You do not have to do any of these things, but some may be helpful to you.

A Final Word on Budgeting

When setting your budget, you need to be realistic about the book's cost to publish and sales goals. This budgeted number is not only the limit to your spending, but it will also become your break-even point.

The break-even point on any published work is the total amount of money spent getting to that point plus any additional marketing costs. Only after sales have netted you enough money to reach that break-even point does your book actually start making money.

Take a good look at the genre you write and the market for your books. Look at their price points and at how those other books are selling. Amazon's sales ranks are an excellent tool to tell you if a book is selling well or not. While not an actual number of sales, the rank can tell you some basic information about how well a book is selling compared to others in the marketplace. Essentially, the lower the number, the better the book is selling. Books that are ranked in the top 2,000 or better are generally selling at least 8-10 books a day, which is a respectable number for an independent author. Anything at that level or below is selling quite well.

You can also talk with other indie authors. They are your best resource for getting a clear picture of how long it took them to establish regular sales and reach their break-even point.

If you've done the market research and talked with other independent authors within your genre, you should have an idea of what you can expect, and then you can factor that into your budget before you get started on the actual production of your book.

Making a Book

Book Production

To make a book you must start with a complete and polished manuscript.

I know what you're thinking, "Thank you, Captain Obvious," but hey, if you aren't finished with this step, you're not ready to self-publish. Actually, your book should have been through multiple revisions and rounds through a critiquing group before you even consider self-publishing.

Self-publishing originally received its dirty image because of the lack of quality associated with it. In the early days of self-publishing, access to quality editors was expensive. Authors who couldn't afford good editing couldn't produce a nice clean product. That reflected badly on the author and self-publishing in general.

Poor quality is the mark of death for your manuscript. So, the first thing you need to do is make sure your manuscript has been through critiquing, beta reading, and proofing before you hire an editor.

That's right, you still need to hire an editor, but only after you have completed the above steps.

Getting Your Work Critiqued

What is a critique? A critique is a thorough review that high-lights both the areas that need improvement as well as the good elements of a written or produced work.

Once you've finished your first draft, it's time to find a part-ner or group of people to help you critique your work. This is an important first step in the process to producing a quality book.

A good critique of your work will help to highlight areas to improve such as grammar, punctuation, plot inconsistencies, incomplete character arcs, unbelievable situations (fiction might be fake, but it has to be believable), etc. Along with areas to improve, a good critique can also highlight areas that are working well within your story.

Every critiquing partnership is different. You could work with a single partner at a time or work within a group setting. Both types of critiquing relationships can be beneficial. It's up to you to decide which ones are right for you.

To find potential critiquing partners or groups, start by looking at other authors. Join writing groups, go to conferences, or become active in online writing communities. Build relationships with others who are doing the same things you are. Once you've established trust with other writers, you can begin to discuss exchanging chapters or manuscripts. If you are looking for something more ready-made, consider some online critiquing workshop sites. My favorite of those is **http://www.critiquecircle.com**.

On a site like Critique Circle, critiquing is generally a chapter-by-chapter review of your work. Other authors read individual chapters on a weekly basis. Just like with a critiquing partner, they will point out parts to tighten, what doesn't make sense, where the plot needs more development, pacing issues, character inconsistencies, and so on.

Most critiquing workshop sites work on a tit-for-tat basis. This means they critique your work, and in exchange, you critique the works of others. While at first you might find this to be added work, it's actually an essential step for you as an author. By critiquing others, you learn to spot mistakes in your own writing.

The critiquing phase is where you will spend the most time. During the critiquing phase, your manuscript should go through various drafts and rewrites. When you've finished here, it should look noticeably different from the original draft you started with.

Proofing Your Work

After critiquing and rewriting your manuscript, take another pass at it to make sure it is clean.

1) Print it! I can't explain why, but seeing something in print somehow makes you look at it a little differently. I can spend hours staring at a computer screen, reading my work, and still miss things. As soon as I see it on paper, I find more errors.

QUICK & DIRTY TIP!

Printing a 300+ page manuscript is costly and wasteful. Try to print double-sided where you can, but don't try to go single spaced. Trust me, your eyes will thank you for that. And set your printers to "fast draft" mode.

2) Read out loud! When we read silently, especially our own work, our brain plays tricks on us. We know what we meant to say, and our brain substitutes the correct sentence or words in for the ones we might have goofed on. Reading out loud stops your brain from this sort of "auto correct" function. You'll find lots more errors this way.

QUICK & DIRTY TIP!

Try having the computer read to you. Sounds kind of silly, but it will definitely help you pick out any problems. Look for free software to help you do this like Natural Reader.

3) Have someone else read it! Hey, sometimes we're just blind to our own mistakes. A fresh set of eyes works wonders. When you have agonized enough over your own words, toss your work to some friends to read. I bet they still find things for you to fix.

4) Have someone read it aloud to you. You'll hear if they "get it."

Beta Readers

Beta readers offer a fresh set of eyes. They are not editors, nor are they a critiquing partner. Think of them as the "focus group" for your manuscript. They are the final step before you move on to an editor. Beta readers are the people who will tell you, after all the revisions, if the overall story works.

Don't rely on just one, though. Not all beta readers are alike. Everybody has different strengths and weaknesses when it comes to reading. Some are better with flow and feel. Some are sticklers for the rules. Some are just good at responding (like laughing when they are supposed to).

Once you've been through this phase, you'll probably have a few more things to clean up, after which you can move on to editing.

Editing

In the traditional publishing world, editing is taken care of by multiple people.

1. **Substantive/developmental editor**. This editor reads the book and tells the author what parts to tighten, what doesn't make sense, what plot threads need to be developed, and so on.

2. **Line editor**. This editor notes grammar issues, redundancies, punctuation issues, and awkward sentence structure.

3. **Copy editor**. This editor intensively edits for continuity as well as grammar and spelling.

4. **Proofreader**. This editor does a final read-through for errors.

If you've followed the steps up to now, you'll already have a few of these essential editing steps covered. That doesn't mean you can skip the editing, it just means your manuscript is that much cleaner to start with.

- A good critiquing group or circle can take care of much of numbers 1 and 2. As I said before, critiquing groups generally work chapter by chapter, and because they work more slowly, they are usually great for spotting the nitty-gritty stuff. They'll call out your plot holes, character inconsistencies, and things like that.

- Beta readers read your book and essentially proof it for obvious errors, covering numbers 1 and 2 again.

- A freelance editor is your last step towards cleaning up your manuscript. Do not skip this step! The failure of many self-published books is due to lack of proper editing.

There are wide varieties of freelance editors out there, and with a little research, you can find one right for you.

> ## QUICK & DIRTY TIP
>
> A wonderful resource to start with is: Predators and Editors
> **http://pred-ed.com/**.
> Think of them as the Consumer Reports for writing resources.

Here is a small list of my personal favorites (editors I have worked with on prior novels).

Sharazade's Editorial Service -
http://sharazade.fannypress.com/

A development editor and copy editor with over ten years of experience, including three years in-house with a New York publishing firm. Experienced with publishers and independent authors, fiction and non-fiction (including academic work).

Editing by Susan Helene Gottfried
http://westofmars.com/west-of-mars/susans-editing-services/

With a BA in English Writing (journalism, PR, and fiction) from the University of Pittsburgh, and an MFA in Creative Writing (Fiction) from Bowling Green State University, Susan has the skills necessary to copy edit or proofread your work.

Red Adept Editing Service
http://redadeptreviews.com/

If you're an indie, you know about their book reviews. Recently, they decided to open up into editing too.

Autumn J. Conley
http://www.facebook.com/pages/Autumn-J-Conley-Proofreader-and-Copy-Editor/133806322428

Proofreader & Copy Editor

Victory Editing
http://victoryediting.com/
A Variety of manuscript services including "Oops Detection" (final proofing).

When you hire a freelance editor, this person should take care of the final copyediting. A good freelance editor will always offer you a sample edit first. A sample edit usually comprises the first five pages of your manuscript. You'll send this to the prospective editor, who will edit that portion for free. This allows you to see the editor's style, as well as let you know how well you would work together. Don't use a freelance editor who doesn't offer a free sample. Once you hire your editor, you can expect him or her to take a thorough pass through your completed manuscript. (Mine generally runs a two-pass approach.) You should receive back an edited manuscript full of notes. In most cases, you'll go back and correct things based on the notes and resubmit to them for a final review. This allows the editor to take one final look over the cleaner manuscript, and if necessary, make any last minute tweaks before sending it back. After this process is completed, your manuscript should be very clean.

At that point, you could send it to another beta reader for a final read through which covers a final "proofing."

Now you're ready to move on to the publishing part of self-publishing.

Main Publishing Formats: Print and Ebook

Deciding on Format, Printing, and Distribution

Once you have a manuscript ready to be published, you're going to have to decide how to publish it. Will it be a print book, an ebook, or both? (Audio is another option, but we won't be getting into that in this book.)

Figure this out before you move on to further steps. Many self-publishers start with ebooks and move into print, but you can also do them both at once.

If you're just concerned with ebook publishing, skip this section (head over to Book Cover Design), as it will deal specifically with the print options. I'll tackle the ebook publishing information in later chapters.

If you chose to go with print, you'll also have to choose the method of delivery. There are two basic flavors here: Offset and POD (Print on Demand).

Offset Printing:

A printing method used to produce large volumes of high-quality documents at a single time.

With this method, you'll work with a printer that works in large batches. What that means is, you'll order a set number of books, and the printer will print them in one run and ship them to you.

The benefits of this printing process are:
- High-quality printing
- Lower "per book" costs
- Greater flexibility in paper, color, and trim sizes.

The negatives of this printing process are:

- Additional shipping and warehousing costs
- Limited distribution (You are your own distributor in most cases.)
- High initial investment (You pay for the lot of books up-front.)
- Costly error correction (Mistakes mean new print runs and additional costs.)

Reasons to use this method:

Depending on the type of book you're looking to produce, you may need the additional paper, color, and trim options (book sizes) that offset printing can offer you. Let's say you have a full-color book. You'll want the high quality and color options. POD—while good—will not be able to give you the best result here. Let's say you are a public speaker, and you use your book (generally nonfiction) as a tool at speaking engagements. It's better to have a bulk stock on hand for this, and because of the lower "per book" cost, this could save you money in the long run.

Reasons to avoid this method:

The single biggest reason to avoid this method of printing is distribution. Offset printers (generally) do not have links to distribution channels to make it easy for you to get your work onto bookstore shelves. Warehousing and shipping cost aside, the distribution is where you, the independent publisher, make money or not. People buying books aren't going to hunt you down. They go to their usual place, be it bookstore or online, and look at the bookshelves. If you're not there, they won't buy your book. Without some kind of connection to a distribution channel like Ingram or Baker & Taylor (the two largest wholesale suppliers of multimedia, books, and related information services to retailers and libraries) to get your book onto shelves, customers aren't going to see your work. In most cases, your books will be in your garage or storage unit, and you'll be the one going to each bookstore to request they shelve your work.

POD – Print On Demand

A printing technology and business process in which new copies of a book are not printed until an order has been received.

At one point in time, POD had a bad reputation for quality. It was thought of as quick and dirty. Today, however, that has changed. Most small press publishers (and even some larger ones) now use POD technology to print books because it's more economical. What POD means is that your book isn't printed until someone orders it (it's printed "on demand"). Because it does not exist (in a physical form) until someone buys it, there is no need for additional warehousing costs.

The benefits of this printing process are:
- No warehousing costs
- Lower initial investment (You pay setup fees instead of bulk buying.)
- Error correcting is easy (You can upload new files as needed, and they will replace the file your printer uses to print the next book ordered.)
- Generally linked with a distribution channel (Ingram or Baker & Taylor)

The negatives of this printing process are:
- Higher "per book" costs
- Limited choice in paper, colors, and trim size

Reasons to use this method:

With a lower initial investment (only having to pay setup fees), your book is cheaper to create. Add to that the benefit of belonging to a distribution network, like Ingram, and your book will also have instant visibility. I use Lightning Source for my printer, and through their network, my books are available at Barnes & Noble and Amazon with no additional setup. Lightning also offers you placement in the UK and Europe with just a click of the mouse. That puts my books in places where readers might be looking. We'll discuss the two big competitive printers further in a later chapter. The main point I'm making here is that easy access, lower setup, and visibility will make your job easier. You still have a lot of work to do, but this option is probably best if you're just starting out.

Printing & Distribution

Unless you plan on going door-to-door with a stack of books, you want a printer who can distribute to the big guys.

The two major players in the self-publishing realm for printing and distribution are Createspace and Lightning Source. TextStream has recently come online and may become yet another power player, but for now, we will just focus on these two.

Lightning Source

Lightning Source (**http://www.lightningsource.com/** a member of the Ingram family of companies) is a major POD printer that is linked with a variety of distribution channels. They are not a publisher. They will also not work with individual authors (this is where setting yourself up as a DBA or LLC is handy). Lightning Source does not do any hand-holding, nor do they offer any paid creative services such as cover design, interior formatting, or layout. With Lightning, you are expected to follow their guidelines and provide them with print-ready covers and interiors as well as the individual ISBNs for your books.

While it may seem daunting at first, the interior layout and setup of print-ready PDF book covers and interiors is not impossible for the DIY self-publisher. It takes a little learning, but it can be done. I'll cover interior design in a later chapter.

Using Lightning Source and its vast distribution network means that when your files are complete and uploaded, they will automatically place your book with Ingram's distribution network. This gives your book maximum visibility.

Being included in the distribution network means seamless product integration. Simply put, when a customer sees your book available on Amazon, for example, they can buy it directly from that Website. Behind the scenes, via the distribution network, the order is sent to Lightning, who then prints and ships the book.

Lightning Source Distribution Partners (there is no guarantee to be listed in all catalogues):

US:
Ingram
Amazon.com
Baker & Taylor
Barnes & Noble
NACSCORP
Espresso Book Machine

UK:
Adlibris.com
Amazon.co.uk
Bertrams
Blackwell
Book Depository
Coutts
Gardners
Mallory International
Paperback Shop
Eden Interactive Ltd.
Aphrohead
I.B.S - STL U.K

To participate in the distribution channels, you will have to allow a discount on your books. Retailers don't pay full price for your book; they want to make a little profit as well. Offering them a discount on your book is incentive for them to include you in their catalog. That way, when a book is sold, everyone gets a cut of the profits. As long as you set your discount within industry standards, your books will be included in the various retailers' catalogs. The minimum discount to participate in these channels is 20% for some and 25% for others. It's best to use 25% across the board to avoid being opted out of any online outlets. In other words, in exchange for being placed on Amazon (for example), you give them a discount on the cost of your book.

You can go as high as you like with the discount, but I would not suggest any lower than 25%.

A side note for those of you wanting to be stocked on bookstore shelves: The minimum discount required for Barnes & Noble to consider your book for their stores is 50%. We'll touch on that subject a little later.

To set up your files with Lightning will cost you $35 for the interior book block and $35 for the cover. These files are separate items that you will upload into the Lightning Source database. Additionally, you will pay a $12 yearly fee to maintain your files in the distribution network. Once those fees are paid, your book is ready to go into production.

There is one other additional fee you may consider paying: Proof $30 (recommended before putting your book into production.) This is a copy that will be sent via overnight delivery (the $30 pays for shipping as well) to you before the book goes into production. This gives you an example of what customers are going to get when they purchase your book. This proof copy is your opportunity to have a final look before it goes into production. Consider this your last chance to fix any errors.

Once your book goes into production, the amount you receive per book will be the total, minus the discount and printing cost (book printing costs are determined by size and page count). These costs are outlined in the contract you sign with Lightning Source prior to book setup. The remainder after those costs will be your individual profit.

Lightning Source also offers short run printing for those who wish to purchase a bulk stock of their books. Like offset printing, this will give you a stock of books to sell, but using their POD system, you do not need to order thousands of books at a time. Short run orders can range from one book to as many books as you like. The cost will vary depending on quantity.

Createspace

Unlike Lightning, who will only work with established companies (this is where creating a DBA or LLC comes in handy), Createspace deals directly with you, the author, to create a book. Createspace offers many services that can be useful and helpful (for a fee). This truly differentiates Createspace from Lightning. Where Lightning operates as only a printer and link to distribution channels, Createspace also acts as a publisher by offering additional services such as an ISBN provider, cover designer, editor, etc. You do not have to choose these options. In fact, if you are the DIY type, you could use Createspace to produce your book for next to nothing.

Setting up through Createspace will be very similar to setting up with Lightning. You will have to create a book block, interior layout, and have your cover file ready. You can use your own ISBN or purchase one from their stock. Unlike Lightning, however, if you have questions or problems, they will be there to help you. Lightning expects you to know what you are doing; Createspace offers ways to help you (some of which cost money). For the beginner, this might be a good way to dip your toe in and see how things work.

Publishing with Createspace, an Amazon company, means your book will be automatically included in their online store. They too have a large distribution network; however, they do not offer the same discounting control that Lightning does. Where Lightning gives you the choice on how low or high to set the discount, Createspace dictates how much of a discount you must give. To opt into their extended distribution network, you will have to offer a 60% discount to Createspace. While that is significantly higher than I recommended with Lightning, I should note that the 60% discount only counts for sales through Createspace's extended distribution network. It does not count for sales via the Createspace eStore (20% discount) or through Amazon.com (40% discount).

Just like with Lightning, the % discount is taken off of the book's cover price, and your royalty is calculated based on that number minus the printing cost of the book. The remainder is what you will be paid.

No matter what you choose, you want to have your printer selected before you move on to further steps in the book process. Each printer will require things to be formatted specifically for them. They will also tell you what trim sizes and paper selections you can use. This information will be extremely helpful when moving on to cover design and book layout.

The Print Book Layout

The layout, otherwise known as the interior book block, is the process of formatting your manuscript so that it will look how you want it to when printed. This includes details such as:

- headers
- footers
- font
- page breaks
- page size
- margins,
- chapter titles

Formatting can be done in Microsoft Word (or whatever word processor you happen to be working with), but it is quite a frustrating process. Also, remember that each different format (ebook, softcover, and hardcover) you choose will have different layout requirements (see your printer's FAQ's for specifics). Before you finish this step and move on to the next, you'll want to know how to do the layout for each respective format.

Ebook
Softcover
Hardcover

As a cost saving tip, I'd suggest dropping the hardcover version for your first attempt. Ebook and softcover are plenty.

So, what should the interior of book look like, and how does it differ from your word-processed manuscript?

Grab a book off your nearest bookshelf and take a look at it. Notice how:

- the headers alternate between pages

- the page numbers are spaced
- different fonts are used
- chapter pages lack both page numbers and headers
- there's a nifty extra-large capital letter at the beginning of the first chapter paragraph (called a "drop cap")
- chapters start on the right page only.

These are just a few of the things that need to be set up during the layout stage of book design.

As a self-publisher, you're already fighting an uphill battle. Though your book might be the next *Twilight* or *Hunger Games*, it will already start off with a stigma because you self-published it. Though self-publishing or indie publishing are becoming much more mainstream, they still have not garnered the prestige of their traditionally published counterparts. What that means for you, the self-published author, is that you must do that much more to make sure your book is indistinguishable, in quality, from others on the bookshelf.

To nail down what your book should look like inside, you need to look at its peer. Take ten or so traditionally published books from your genre and go through them with a fine-tooth comb. Note the standards in their layout so you can try to mimic them. Also, please note that fiction books differ from non-fiction in the way their interiors are set up.

So, now that you know what a book should look like, how do you recreate it?

On paper, it sounds pretty easy. Change a few fonts here, create some page breaks there, and add in a few page numbers; then *poof*, you have a bright shiny new book!

Once you actually try to duplicate what you see in printed books, you find out how difficult it can be.

While Microsoft Word is great for general word processing, it can be very difficult to use when formatting books. Trying to get page numbers to show up on some pages but not others will provide a bit of a challenge. Same goes for alternating headers that only appear within chapters but not on title pages, acknowledgement pages, "about the author" pages, or copyright pages. Drop cap doesn't ever work as it was intended, and usually adds extra spacing to your lines. In short, it creates a lot of headaches.

Even though it's a headache, book layout can be done on a word processor. It is, however, going to be a frustrating and time-consuming process. Be prepared for long hours. For the do-it-yourself publisher, this is going to be your cheapest option.

There are other alternatives if you don't want to deal with the added stress. For those choosing to use a service, Lulu, CreateSpace, and many others offer layout and design as part of their packages. You can also hire out for this. There are many companies out there who specialize in layout. This will cost you some money—between $100 - $400, and maybe even more.

Self-Pub.net offers some affordable options ranging from $99 - $299, depending on the level of detail needed in your book (nonfiction is generally more labor intensive and costs more).
http://www.self-pub.net/layout/

Rising Sign Books also offers some formatting and layout services. Prices start at $100 for basic interiors.
http://www.risingsignbooks.net/p/services.html

There are also many programs that professional typographers and graphic designers use (Quark and InDesign come to mind). They are available for anyone to use, but they will cost between $699 - $1,000. I was lucky enough to stumble across a program that works within Microsoft Word. I found this program on Self-pub.net (who as I stated above also offers formatting services), and it was quite helpful and only cost around $40.

http://www.self-pub.net
Book Design Wizard 2.0
*Not compatible with Mac computers.

This program standardizes things for you via pre-coded (VBA) templates. You answer some questions about your book and plug in your layout desires (e.g., what fonts to use for chapter headings, title pages, and so on), and it creates a template in a separate Word document for you to work within.

I found the Book Design Wizard to be extremely helpful. It still took me a little while to learn the software and get the book layout exactly as I wanted it, but in the end, my books are now formatted exactly like their traditionally published counterparts. I can now format a print-ready book block in just a couple of hours' time. For the do-it-yourselfer, this is probably the best happy medium you'll find. I'm sure this is not the only program of its kind out there. You can do a Google search for book layout templates and programs. If you don't like this one, you can probably find another to suit your needs.

Some basic tips for proper interior formatting:

- **Start all chapters on the right page**.
  Not all publishers do this, but it does help provide some nice uniformity to your work. Ensuring that all chapters begin on the same side keeps things neat and tidy. It will result in the occasional blank page, so consider that in your costs. Generally speaking, POD printers charge by the page, so doing this could result in a few more cents per book.
- **Page numbers don't go on every page**.
  In most novels, page numbers are excluded from title pages, copyright pages, additional information pages (like "about the author"), and chapter openers. Don't make the mistake of leaving your page numbers everywhere; it will make your work look unprofessional. Also, along with remembering what pages get what numbers, remember that odd-number pages are always on the right.

- **Headers don't go on every page**.
  Just like with page numbers, headers and footers do not appear on every page. Make sure your headers are only on pages where they are needed.
- **Justify your work**.
  In print novels, ragged right margins are not acceptable. You want a nice and uniform look to your words. Never forget to properly align your text.

Bookstore Shelves

Is it really worth the effort?

One of the things we authors dream of is seeing our book on store shelves. This can be done with both Lightning and Createspace, but let me give you some honest facts about the cost-effectiveness of this dream.

With Lightning, you are given a print cost based on your book size and page count. You then have to set the discount for the distribution channel. Your royalties back are based on the remainder.

Originally I tried to get onto store shelves. This was a costly mistake. Here's why.

Let's say, for argument's sake, you want to charge $10.00 per book. The book is roughly 300 pages. Let's say the print cost is $4.50 for a 5x8 book, standard cream-colored paper, and color cover. (Please note that actual print costs will be outlined in the contract you sign with your printer, I am only offering approximate prices here for example purposes.)

Each of these books will cost $4.50 to print.

To get into the distribution channels you are required to set a minimum discount of 25%. So that's $2.50.

$10.00 (retail) minus $4.50 (printing) minus $2.50 (distribution discount) = $3.00

You'll make three dollars on every book sold.

Now to get onto store shelves at Barnes & Noble, you have to offer the industry standard discount, which is 55%. On a $10.00 book, that's $5.50.

$10.00 (retail) minus $4.50 (printing) minus $5.50 (distribution discount) = $0.00

That means you need to increase the price of the book in order to make even the smallest profit.

Let's try $15.00 ($8.25 = 55% discount)

$15.00 (retail) minus $4.50 (printing) minus $8.25 (distribution discount) = $2.25

With the average price of paperback books ranging from $7.99 (pocket size in bookstores) to $9.99 (indie books average), $15.00 sticks out like a sore thumb. Remember, you're trying to be competitive here. For fiction, a $15.00 price is not going to look as attractive to buyers when there are a lot of cheaper options out there.

Also, there is no guarantee major bookstores will stock your books. Just to be approved by their sales department, you have to set the discount to market standards (55%), then query them and provide a complete marketing plan for the books. (We will discuss marketing plans in a later chapter.)

Barnes & Noble
Small Press Department, 122 Fifth Avenue
New York, New York, 10011.

BooksAMillion
Director of Merchandising, Booksamillion.com,
P.O. Box 19728
Birmingham, AL 35219

Then, if/when they finally approved your book, they may order only a few to test the market. You have to prove that your book will sell to keep them buying it.

QUICK & DIRTY TIP!

If you really want to see your books on store shelves, set your discount as low as it will go and then do the legwork to find independent stores willing to shelve you. It will be more cost-effective, and you will still live the dream of being in a bookstore.

Independent book stores, on the other hand, are generally more than willing to stock your book on a consignment basis. If you purchase your own stock of books and bring them to the bookstore, they will generally work out some kind of an arrangement with you.

Book Cover Design

What makes a good book cover?

Let's face it: People do judge a book by its cover. Book browsers will only give a book a few seconds' glance. A good cover can draw potential readers in, whereas a poorly designed cover can send them running for the hills.

This is what drives many people to pay an artist hundreds of dollars to do a cover for them. I'm not saying that's wrong. Just please remember your budget.

Your cover should do three things: Advertise the book, showcase the author, and set the "feel" of the book.

That's the first thing people are going to see when they look at your work. So it goes without saying that your cover needs to be an attention-grabber. It needs to stand out among thousands of other books within its genre.

If your book catches a reader's eye, it might get them to read the back cover (in a store) or product description (for online shopping). Beyond that, they may take a chance on a sample (online) or decide to buy the book right there. And that's exactly what you want.

Remember this when thinking of cover design: It's the most important visual sales tool you have, and it's worth spending a little extra time and a few extra dollars here. Cover art and editing are the two places where most of your budget will be spent (marketing being the remainder).

For most of us, cover art is something we will have to hire out for. We're writers; that doesn't mean we're graphic artists. "Don't quit your day job." It's okay to NOT be a graphic artist. If you don't have the skills necessary to produce a professional-looking book cover, then you'll need to get in touch with a freelance artist.

There are a wide variety of freelance graphic artists available who can produce a beautiful cover. Prices, however, will vary depending on the artist, so shop around. One thing to consider when looking for artists: You want someone who specializes in book cover art. Not all artists are suited for working on book covers. Here are a couple of my personal favorites:

Willsin's World – Book covers & trailers
http://www.willsinrowe.blogspot.com/

Phatpuppy Art – Beautiful artwork available for purchase and use as book covers.
http://phatpuppyart.com/

Those are just a couple of the many designers out there. Do your research and ask around to find your designers. Social networking sites like Facebook are wonderful for this; there are lots of groups out there of aspiring novelists, and they have a wealth of information and leads.

Once you've hired a designer, there is one more important thing to remember. In most cases, you are purchasing rights to use their artwork. The art may not be yours and yours alone. You'll need to know if those are exclusive rights, or if they are just general rights of use.

"Exclusive rights" means you are the only one that will be able to use that picture. Exclusive rights may have some limitations on them. In some cases, there are time limits. You may have rights of exclusivity for a year or more, or you may have permanent exclusive rights. This is an important thing to consider when paying someone to create your cover. You don't want to spend your hard-earned cash only to see someone else with the exact same design a week later.

Tips for working with a cover designer

Look for someone who wants to work with your vision. This is your baby, and the cover is the first thing people will see. Have an idea of what you want and look for someone who can work with your idea. There is nothing worse than working with someone who wants to steamroll your idea with their own because they are an "artist." If the artist is not someone you can work with, no matter how good that person is, they aren't the artist for you.

Along with that, you want to work with someone you are comfortable with. Don't be afraid to ask questions, and most especially, don't be afraid to ask for changes if the artwork they present isn't quite right. Even when hiring an artist, collaboration is key to developing the vision into a stunning piece of art.

Always get things in writing. Even if it's just an email, make sure all details of your agreement are in some form of written communication. This protects both you and the designer from risk. Whenever possible, a "Work for Hire" contract is best, but not all freelancers work with contracts. Having things in writing is a way to ensure that there is no confusion about details, rights, and payment.

Know what you need. Beyond the idea of what kind of art you want, your designer will want to know important details about the specifications about your book. I learned this the hard way. Know your book dimensions before this step. Know the page count, the size of the book, and if you will be publishing in softcover, hardcover, and/or ebook. Do your book layout first. Along with that, know your deadline.

Lastly, make sure your artist takes payment in two parts. This, just like getting everything in writing, protects you both. Half payment should be made when you hire/commission the artist, and the second half should be paid upon delivery of final product. Paying all of the money upon delivery places pressure on the artist to rush to give you the art so they can get paid. Paying all of the money in advance can hurt you as well. It means you are taking a risk that the art will be exactly what you want. In most cases, it will be, but there are some cases where you and the artist might not see eye-to-eye, and once money has changed hands, things get hairy. So, remember, paying in halves is the best way to go.

Tips for DIY cover design

For the true DIY self-publisher, doing your own book cover can be another way to maintain 100% control over the product.

For that, you will have to have 1) the software capable of manipulating photographs, and 2) the knowledge of how to do it.

Now, I won't go into detail there (if you want a Photoshop manual, I'd suggest hopping down to your local bookstore. You can also find many tutorials for other programs online). What I will do, though, is give you some guidelines on the basic elements of a good book cover.

If you're just starting out and want to create ebook-only files, you can download a free program called GIMP.

http://www.gimp.org/

This image manipulation program will help you do the basic things you need to make a cover that can be used for ebooks. It works in RGB (Red Green Blue) only, so it will not be able to create your print book files, which require CMKY (Cyan, Magenta, Key [black], and Yellow). Along with that, you may also want to look at Inkscape (**http://inkscape.org/**), which is similar to Adobe Illustrator.

For print-ready files, though, you might need something a little more powerful. The most popular would be Photoshop.

A book cover contains three basic elements:
- Striking artwork
- A bold book title
- A legible author's name

Let's start with art. The first thing you should ask yourself is: What is my genre?

When picking cover art, you need to use something that fits within the "norm" for your genre. Look at other books and see what overall theme or style they use. For example: Urban fantasy. Lately, the trend in urban fantasy is a kick-ass female on the cover. She's generally in front of part of a city view. How about

Romance? Generally romance covers have a man and woman in an intimate setting with a scenic background. Simple enough, right?

These are the standards, and they give you a jumping-off point for searching out your artwork. You want your readers, who expect a certain look or feel, to know that your book fits with their standards. That does not mean you should copy someone else's cover; it means, rather, that you should use it as a springboard.

Once you have an idea of what you want, you'll need to locate the artwork. There are many places online to find and purchase royalty-free images ("royalty-free" refers to the right to use copyrighted material or intellectual property without the need to pay royalties for each use). Here are a few listings to get you started.

http://bigstockphoto.com
http://shutterstock.com
http://istockphoto.com
http://dreamstime.com
http://fotosearch.com
http://www.romancenovelcovers.com

As you can see, there are a wide variety of royalty-free photos out there for you to purchase. Prices and quality span the ranges through the sites, but if you're willing to spend the time looking, you can come up with some beautiful art.

With the growing popularity of e-books, another important consideration has arisen in regard to cover art. Just as hardcover and softcover books have their own technical requirements, so too do the various electronic reader options. You'll need to make sure your artwork translates to the e-reader screen as well.

For example, many e-readers have only a gray-scale screen. Certain colors (such as red) show up poorly when converted to grays. The same applies to many pastels. You'll need to check out your artwork in a black-and-white or gray scale form before finalizing it. Don't risk alienating readers because you didn't ensure the artwork was compatible.

Along with that, please keep it simple. Many new self-publishers feel the need to make their cover stand out by encompassing every single element possible from the story. Less is more! Some of the best covers out there are ones with simple yet bold statements.

Beyond beautiful artwork, there is also the typography to consider too. Both your title and author name need to be clearly visible to readers. Remember, your cover is the first thing they see. You want to make sure they can clearly distinguish you and your book at first sight.

Things to consider with fonts

1. Organize size of fonts in order of importance. The title of the book should be the largest font on the cover. (At least until you're Stephen King.) Author name should be smaller, but still prominent. Any subsequent text or quotes you wish to add should continue to be smaller in size.

2. Select the color of fonts to stand out, yet still feel like it belongs.

3. Organize the placement of fonts to work with the artwork, not against it. Don't cover up beautiful artwork with your words. Yes, some things will get covered, but you should not plaster a title across the best part of the picture.

4. Don't clutter the cover with text. Only text that is abso-lutely necessary should be there. Quotes are nice, but limit it to one on the cover. Use your interior pages for continued praise of the book.

Pick fonts that are striking and bold enough to be seen in both large and small sizes. You have to account for the people who might pick you up on a store shelf as well as those browsing the virtual racks.

Amazon is one of the biggest ebook retailers. When browsing through their store, customers are viewing book covers that have been shrunk to around 105 x 135 pixels. That's less than half an inch high. If your book cover merely looks plain at that size, you risk potential buyers simply ignoring it. If your cover looks awful, you risk actively repulsing your target market. Picking fonts that are strong enough and clear enough to be read at this size is a must!

QUICK & DIRTY TIP

Limit yourself to no more than two fonts on your front cover. You might think it's cute to have different fonts for the title, author name, and various quotes, but trust me, it only makes your cover look amateurish. Stick with one or two fonts for the cover. That includes front, back, & spine.

Once you've got your font picked out, placing it on the cover art can be tricky. You want it to fit nicely within the art or around the art without detracting from it. There is no hard and fast rule when it comes to type placement on book covers; however, there are some things you want to avoid doing.

Don't run your text all the way to the end of the image. In print, you'll end up cutting off part of the title in the bleed area. In ebooks, your title will just look crowded.

As with anything, rules can be broken... but you need to show "just cause." Your book is called *Claustrophobia*? Then it might just work to have the title crammed in all the way to the edges of the cover, even slightly outside it. But if it's going to print, rather than just electronic, you'd have to check with your printer. A requirement like that is outside the standard, and so may incur an extra cost.

Again, these are guidelines not hard and fast rules. If you plan to do it yourself, take your time to really figure out what works and what doesn't. Make a few mockups and get peer reviews before you go to print.

Print Book vs. Ebook Covers

Print covers and ebook covers are different breeds of the same animal. An ebook cover is a single picture—essentially the front cover of the book—whereas the print cover encompasses three parts that all must work in unison. With print books, you need to have that front image (just like your ebook cover) as well as a back image and a spine.

Your spine measurements will be determined by your printer's specs, using size of the book, paper weight, and page count. Your front and back images will also have sizing requirements based on the height and width of your book.

Each of these pieces will need to fit together like a puzzle. The combination of all three will create your cover file image.

If you are going to be working in both print and ebook, you'll have to make sure your cover artist knows the specifications for your printer. They'll need to create two separate files, one for the ebook and one for the print book.

If you're going to create the book cover yourself, pay very close attention to your printer's specifications when it comes to creating the print book cover. Each company will have different requirements for sizing and ink weights. Also, remember that printers use CMKY (Cyan, Magenta, Key [black], and Yellow) color instead of RGB (Red, Green, Blue), which is used for computer images.

Copyright

Let's pause for a moment in our discussion of book production and talk about a few key things you should do before you go to print.

Copyright: The author's legal right to ownership of the work under federal copyright laws.

Just by writing it, your book is covered under copyright protection. However, without filing your registration, you'll find it very difficult to enforce.

I'm sure you've heard of the "poor man's copyright" before. If not, it's the process of printing and mailing yourself a complete copy of your finished manuscript so you can prove by the postmark when it was created. This may show when you created and finalized the work, but it does not give you the official registration of the Library of Congress, nor can it be easily used to show proof when sending "cease and desist" letters.

The burden of proof is 100% in your hands, and to enforce it, you'll have to take your matter to court without the ability to claim any attorney's fees.

If you file your claim properly, and register your work in a timely manner, you are protected. Registering your copyright establishes a public record of your "rights of authorship." There is no burden of proof on who owns the work; it is officially yours.

In today's digital age, you'll need that official proof of copyright if you want to issue a "DCMA (Digital Millennium Copyright Act) takedown notice" (a written notification of claimed infringement) to remove pirated copies of your work from Websites.

You can easily file your Copyright online. It only costs $35. You can also pre-register your work if you feel it is necessary; however, the costs are much higher for this. (This is only recommended if you are sharing your pre-published work with people and fear it being stolen.)

http://www.copyright.gov/

Once the copyright is filed, your book is officially protected from copyright infringement. Please note: It will take between four and six months for the official form from the Library of Congress to arrive, but even with the delay in paperwork, your work is protected from the moment you hit "submit."

Piracy

The term "piracy" is used to describe the act of unauthorized selling, manufacturing, and/or distributing of work copyrighted to someone else.

Many new indie authors are afraid of epublishing because of piracy.

While it is a legitimate fear, it's one that you'll have to get over pretty quickly. If your book is out in the public marketplace, and popular enough that people are going to want to buy it, someone will pirate it. It's going to happen with both print and ebooks. Don't let the fear of pirating stop you from taking your books digital.

I'm not trying to downplay the effect of piracy. It does affect independent authors directly. People who pirate our work do not know the effort we put into it, nor do they care that it was our hard-earned money spent to produce it. All they know is, they see a book and find a way to get it for free. That free copy equates to a lost sale. As an indie, you will feel that loss.

However, not having that ebook out there will equate to many, many more lost sales.

As I said above, ebooks are where the money's at. Because of their low price, readers are more willing to buy ebooks and take a chance on a new author. That means more people are willing to buy your book.

There are ways to help combat piracy, but not all of them are recommended.

Just like CDs in the music industry, ebooks come with the option of adding DRM (Digital Rights Management). DRM is a type of access control method employed to ensure that the copy you licensed is not transferred to another person or device.

When you purchase a print book, it's yours to do with as you please. You can share it with others, read it as many times as you want, or even sell it to someone else. You own that physical copy. With ebooks, you don't actually own anything. It's a digital copy that you essentially license to use from whichever publishing vendor you purchased it from.

When you upload your book to Amazon, you are given the option to add DRM or not. You'll probably be tempted to apply the DRM. Don't.

While the idea behind DRM is good, and it helps slow down digital pirates (let's face it, they know how to crack DRM—you're not stopping them, you're just slowing them down for a few minutes), it also prevents paying customers from being able to transfer the book they purchased among their own reading devices. This can put readers off of purchasing your book, and that is something you do not want to do.

While you can't prevent piracy, you can take some steps to protect yourself from it. Firstly, make sure your book is protected by copyright. With copyright protection in place, you can easily go after any Websites that may be pirating your work.

QUICK & DIRTY TIP

Google Alerts
http://www.google.com/alerts
Utilize this tool to let you know any time that your book title comes up online. This will alert you to any buzz about your book, as well as tell you when it appears on torrents or other places where people can download it for free.

If your book comes up on any pirate Websites, then you can send a DCMA Takedown Notice with your copyright information. It's the equivalent of a "cease and desist" notice. The DMCA states that while an Internet Service Provider (ISP) is not liable for transmitting information that may infringe a copyright, the ISP must remove materials from users' websites that appear to constitute copyright infringement after receiving proper notice.

A DCMA Takedown Notice must:

- Be in writing.
- Be signed by the copyright owner or agent. An electronic signature is acceptable.
- Identify the copyrighted work that you claim has been infringed.
- Identify the type or method of infringing on your work.
- Include you or a registered agent of the copyright holder's contact info.
- State that you are complaining in "good faith."
- State "under penalty of perjury, that the information contained in the notification is accurate."
- State that you have the right to proceed (because you are the copyright owner or the owner's agent).

Once sent, your files should be removed from the infringing Website within 24 hours.

ISBNs

ISBN (International Standard Book Number): An ISBN is your publishing "social security number." It is a 13-digit string of numbers that identifies the book, the publisher, and what format the material is in: ebook, softcover, hardbound, or audio.

A unique ISBN is required for each format of your book, so you'll have to purchase an ISBN for the various formats you plan on producing.

You can purchase ISBNs in the US at:
www.myidentifiers.com.

I recommend you start off with a block of 10 ISBNs. They are $250, which breaks down to $25 a piece. Comparatively, a single ISBN is $125, so even if you aren't going to use them all they will pay for themselves within a couple of books.

When you purchase your ISBNs, you'll be offered the option of purchasing your barcodes as well. This is an additional fee and not always necessary. If you are working with Lightning as your printer, you will not need to purchase barcodes. This is one of the things they automatically apply to your book. That will save you a few dollars.

A single ISBN is meant to represent a format, not a single title. This means a print version and ebook version of the same title should have different ISBNs. Remember that. Also remember that some ebook formats do not require them. Amazon, for example, will assign its own number, an ASIN—which refers to Amazon's own inventory system. Be sure you look to see which formats will require them and which ones don't. This will prevent you from wasting all of your ISBNs on a single title.

Once you have your ISBN assigned, you can log into Bowker Link, the publisher access system, and maintain your ISBN logbook. This is where you can pre-assign ISBNs for books and update the titles that have already been assigned.
http://www.bowkerlink.com

PCN or LCCN

An LCCN (Library of Congress Catalog Number) and/or PCN (Pre-assigned Control Number) assigns a library cataloging number to your book. It's only necessary if you want to get your print books into libraries.

http://pcn.loc.gov/pcn001.html

There is no charge for an LCCN or a PCN; however, you are obligated to send a complimentary copy of all books for which a LCCN or a PCN was provided immediately upon publication.

Library of Congress
US & Publisher Liaison Division
Cataloging in Publication Program
101 Independence Avenue, S.E.
Washington, D.C. 20540-4283

Putting the Book Together and Proof Acceptance!

Okay, so you've formatted, you've edited, you've obtained a cover design and a layout to match each media format. You've purchased your ISBNs and filed your copyright. You're ready to squish it all together and make a book.

This is where the printer comes in.

If you followed your printer's instructions, you will have files to upload for each format. This is where the fun happens. All your hard work and effort will finally culminate into something you can physically hold in your hand!

Usually within 48 hours of your upload, you will have the option to generate a proof. Do not skip this step, no matter how "perfect" you think the book is. You need to see that proof. You need to make *sure* the book looks perfect. Once you have that baby in your hot little hands, it's time to go through it with a fine-tooth comb. Once approved, this is what the world will see. It has to be perfect.

- Check the spine—make sure it is even.
- Check the cover design for flaws.
- Check the pages to make sure there is no fading on the ink.
- Make sure the page numbers are correct.
- Verify chapter headings.
- Look for spelling and grammatical mistakes (I bet you still find a few).

On my first proof I found so many problems I had to go back for another round of editing.

Note that each round of revisions will cost you (generally the cost to revise an interior book block or cover image is equal to the original setup fee for that file; e.g. $35-$40 per file type), so try to catch everything you can!

You will probably never catch all mistakes. I have already had people point out the mistakes in my new release. Thankfully there aren't too many. This is one of the downsides to self-publishing. You don't have a team of people hunting for each and every mistake. Try to make sure your book is as perfect as can be before you approve it.

Ebook Publishing

Now that we've talked about the print side of self-publishing, we can move on to the other format: ebooks. Technically speaking, an ebook encompasses three major formats.

Before I jump into the how-to of ebook formatting, I want to take a moment to give you a little background info. Ebooks, though a major format in book publishing, are still growing and changing. Unlike with the music industry, which has a standardized format, ebooks come in a variety of different formats (mobi, ePub, LRF) for the various e-readers on the market, as well as text and PDF for computer viewing. Eventually, there will be one dominant format, but until that time, self-publishers will need to learn to cope with the three major formats: mobi (Kindle), ePub (Nook & Sony), and PDF (computer).

Ebooks are where indie authors make their money.

Creating an ebook sounds like a daunting task, but while yes, it is time consuming, it is not impossible to do, even for the true neophyte.

To start, let's take a quick look at the three big choices (already on the market) when considering to self-publish your ebooks.

Amazon, the largest of the e-retailers and home of the very popular Kindle, allows you to create a free account with their KDP service.

https://kdp.amazon.com

You can publish your ebook for free, and depending on the price you set, you will receive 35-70% royalties.

• For books priced at $0.99 to $2.98, you will receive 35% on the sale of each book.

• For books priced at $2.99 to $9.99, you will receive 70% on the sale of each book.

• For books priced above $9.99 the royalty rate is reduced back to 35%.

This is Amazon/Kindle's way of helping to keep ebooks priced lower than their printed counterpart.

Kindle does require a little know-how on formatting, but there are a variety of free resources out there to help you do this. You may have heard me mention MobiPocket Creator before.

http://www.mobipocket.com/en/downloadsoft/productdetails creator.asp

Barnes & Noble, home of the Nook, another "big guy" in the ebookseller world. They recently started their own self-publishing venture called PubIt!

http://pubit.barnesandnoble.com

Very similar to Amazon's KDP service, PubIt! allows you to upload an already formatted ePub file. This makes it available for sale on Barnes and Noble's Nook e-reader. According to the PubIt! Website, they have no initial setup fees and pay royalties of 40-65%, depending on the starting price of the book.

• For books priced at $0.99 to $2.98, you will receive 40% on the sale of each book.

• For books priced at $2.99 to $9.99, you will receive 65% on the sale of each book.

• For books priced above $9.99, the royalty rate is reduced back to 40%.

Just like with Amazon/Kindle, this is done to help keep ebook prices low.

http://pubit.barnesandnoble.com

Again, just like with Kindle, a little know-how is needed to properly format a book for ePub; but again there is a wealth of information out there.

The third major player I want to talk about in self-publishing ebooks is **Smashwords**.

https://www.smashwords.com/

Just like with Amazon KDP and Pubit!, there are no setup fees to get your books into virtual print. There are, however, very specific formatting guidelines to upload your Word document that you'll have to follow in order for their Meatgrinder service to adapt your manuscript to all reader devices. That is the major difference between this publisher and the last two. Just as distribution is key in print, the same applies for ebooks as well. Smashwords will ensure that your ebook is available to a wide audience via the multiple formats it creates:

Online Reading (HTML)

Online Reading (JavaScript)

Kindle (.mobi)

ePub (open industry format, good for Stanza reader, others)

PDF (good for highly formatted books, or for home printing)

RTF (readable on most word processors)

LRF (for Sony Reader)

Palm Doc (PDB) (for Palm reading devices)

Plain Text (download) (flexible, but lacks much formatting)

Plain Text (view) (viewable as Web page)

Because of their large distribution network, an ISBN is required. Not all ebooks require them. Kindle, for example, has no real use for them. When you publish with Amazon KDP, your book is assigned an ASIN by Amazon.

So, when you publish with Smashwords, you are given the option to use an ISBN that you own or use theirs for free. If you opt for the free ISBN, you will not be listed as the publisher, Smashwords will. You may also opt to pay for a single ISBN through Smashwords for $9.95. The decision on whether to use a free ISBN or not is up to you. If you are setting yourself up as a publisher and going with a DBA or LLC, then I would suggest purchasing and using your own ISBNs so that you are always listed as the publisher of record. Otherwise, it does you no harm to have the book listed with Smashwords as the publisher.

The cost for setting up your book is $0, and your book is automatically made available to:

Barnes & Noble - Nook
Sony
Kobo - Borders eBook store is powered by Kobo
Amazon - Kindle
Apple
Diesel

You will notice that they also distribute to Kindle and Nook; you can opt out of those and still make your book available to all of the other choices. It is recommended that you *do* opt out of distribution through Kindle and Nook and upload with them separately, because it will give you much more control of how those books appear as well as faster royalty payments with those sites. Smashwords pays quarterly, while Amazon KDP and Pubit! pay on a faster schedule.

QUICK & DIRTY TIP

Smashwords allows you to download all of your formats for free. That means once converted, you will have fully functioning ePub and mobi formats. This can become helpful to have when sending off ebooks for review. Do not; however, use these files to upload to Amazon KDP or Pubit! services. They are not as clean as the individual formats you create separately.

Those are the three Websites you'll definitely want to hit when you self-publish your ebook. Other websites you might want to consider are:

All Romance Ebooks
http://www.allromanceebooks.com/
Book Strand
http://www.bookstrand.com/
Fictionwise
http://www.fictionwise.com/

Ebook Layout

Ebooks are completely different from their paper-bound counterparts where formatting and layout are concerned. In some ways, though, ebooks can be easier to format; however, due to the variety of readers on the market, you will have to create various layouts.

In the ebook world, you have two popular formats: ePub and Kindle/MobiPocket. You'll need to create separate formatted documents for these.

Thankfully, formatting for ePub and MobiPocket is pretty easy and can be done with Microsoft Word and the help of some free programs you can find online.

My favorite program for creating Kindle files is:
MobiPocket Creator
*This program is **not** Mac compatible.*
http://www.mobipocket.com/en/downloadsoft/productdetails creator.asp
This easy-to-use creator takes your word document and turns it into a PRC file. This file can be directly uploaded to the Amazon KDP site.
https://kdp.amazon.com

For ePub, there are quite a few options out there. I use Calibre.

This program is Mac compatible

http://calibre-ebook.com/

This easy-to-use creator takes your word document and turns it into a PRC file (for Kindle) as well as an ePub file (for use with Pubit!)

A simple Google search will bring up plenty of other options. Choose whatever works best for you.

To show you a little of what goes into ebook formatting (it's really pretty easy), I'm going to run quickly though the steps using MobiPocket Creator to make a Kindle-ready ebook.

Kindle Formatting

The Kindle format is actually a basic HTML coded document that uses CSS (cascading style sheets). That probably sounds like gobbledygook to you right now, but don't let yourself get intimidated. While there is a small learning curve to Kindle formatting, you can get by and have a nicely formatted book without having to learn a completely new language.

Amazon's KDP site claims to accept HTML, Word, and PDF documents, but you will not achieve the results you want by uploading in those formats. It's best you format for the Kindle specifically, by creating a .PRC file or mobi file.

This can be done with a little HTML know-how and one of many free programs available on the market. I prefer to use MobiPocket Creator for my Kindle files, but another program Calibre is excellent as well. Calibre is also superb at converting your ePub files, which we will discuss later.

Step 1 – Lay out your Word document as you would if you wanted to create a PDF.

- Don't worry about adjusting page sizes; use your standard 8.5x11 page size with 1-inch margins, and leave the text single-spaced.
- Make sure you use page breaks between chapters and initial cover pages.
- Never use page numbers in ebooks. Due to the compression of page size to accommodate the smaller screen, your page numbers will become oddly placed and will not represent the actual page the reader is seeing.

Example Layout:

Page 1 should be your cover image. Insert the image and size it and center it so it takes up the whole page. Make sure it is also set "in line with text," so there is no odd funky formatting when it is converted to HTML.

Page 2 Title and "published by" page

Page 3 Copyright info

Page 4 Acknowledgements

Page 5 Optional title page

Page 6 Start of book (Make sure you use page breaks between chapters.)

Final page(s) About the author & upcoming books

Ebooks may look similar to their print counterparts, but they are vastly different! Do not attempt to take your wonderfully formatted print interior and expect it to transfer smoothly or to look identical to the ebook version. Now, that's not to say the ebook format is inferior in any way, it's just a simpler beast with about 10x the amount of formatting work. Think of it like building a Web page from scratch. Your words will appear exactly where you code them, but that extremely large amount of coding that goes into the background is invisible. That principle applies to ebooks: You have to tell the little e-reader how to display your book. That means there is code behind the scenes that the device is translating for you.

Don't let me scare you away with talk of code. Yes, some simple coding is involved, but you will not have to be a computer genius to make your book available in the e-marketplace.

Step 2: Prep your Word document.

It's always best to start with a clean slate. Before making any changes, save your Word document as FileName-Kindle.doc or whatever naming convention will let you know that this is specifically a Kindle version. Since you will format for at least three different ebook sites, this will help you differentiate the files. This also protects your original document, should you make any mistakes.

Once you have your file saved for the Kindle, you can begin to prep your work for conversion.

Please note that for the following steps I am using MS Word as my word-processing software.

Step 3: Normalizing Text

Normalizing your text simply means making your text nice and uniform. In this step you will be reducing fonts and sizes to just a few simple choices. E-readers cannot handle special fonts, nor can they handle large font sizes well. The simpler you make it in the beginning, the easier a time you will have working through the rest of your layout.

Before you begin, make sure you have your Track Changes turned off. What you will want to have turned on, however (at least for the next few steps) is the Show/Hide feature. It will help you while normalizing text because it lets you see any hidden formatting. The show/hide button in MS Word is that funky little symbol that looks like this ¶

Once clicked, it will show every space between letters, every paragraph return, and more… As I said, it will help you see any previously hidden formatting issues.

Now you're ready to start normalizing your document. Begin with the text first. As I said before, fancy fonts do not work. Simple fonts such as Times New Roman, Garamond, and Arial are recommended.

Ereaders are not like print books, so the simpler you make things the cleaner they will be in the end. The same applies to text size. I recommend using no larger than 14pt for book and chapter titles and 12pt for regular text.

Use "select all" (Ctrl + A) and highlight all text in your document. Now you can adjust your font type and size at the same time. (Don't worry about chapter titles and extras, you'll go back and fix those in a moment.)

While you have it all selected, adjust your spacing as well. Make sure everything is single spaced. A nice way to convert everything together (if you are in Word 2007 or 2010) is to use the styles buttons to define what "normal" text is.

You can accomplish this very easily. With your entire document still highlighted, find the "styles" menu under "Home." Right click on Normal (the first option) and select "Modify."

This is where you will set the template for "Normal." Pay attention because you will need to do this for "Heading 1" as well.

Under "formatting," select your font and your size. Make sure the color is also the standard black. Below that you can set your spacing. Select "single" and be sure your paragraph alignment is set to "Left." You cannot use "Justified" when formatting for ebooks.

At the very bottom you will see one more button, "Format." Click that and select "paragraph." This brings up further spacing options. You've already specified single and left alignment, but there is one last thing to adjust: the line spacing between paragraphs. This should be 0 for both before and after.

Once you have everything selected, apply it. It should now adjust all of your highlighted text.

The next step in normalizing your work is to make sure you have no tabbed indents. These do not play well with any ebook format. One way to remove them is to use Word's "find/replace feature" (Ctrl + H). Search for ^t (that little ^ is called a caret and is the symbol above the number 6) and replace it with nothing. That will run through the entire document and remove any tabbed indents. Once those are gone, you'll need to use your ruler to set the appropriate indent (.25 works well for ebooks, but .50 is good too.).

Step 4: Adding in the Style.

QUICK & DIRTY TIP!

Be sure to save as you go. You've made quite a lot of changes at this point. You don't want to lose them.

Now that your font, size, and paragraph styles have all been normalized, you'll need to go back through and update chapter headings and adjust title pages and your front and back matter.

This is where that little "style" button helps. On the Home tab (MS Word 2007 or higher) you should see more than one style option available. Look for "Heading 1." This will be important for you when you start to make your Table of Contents.

Right click on Heading 1 and set your formatting. I generally use Times New Roman, 14pt black font, and select "centered" for the justification. You'll also want to select the formatting button again at the bottom and define paragraph styles. Remember to set line spacing before and after to 0.

Once you have the format assigned. Go through your document and use this "Heading 1" for the book title, each chapter, and on titles of any important front and back matter (acknowledgement pages and "about the author" pages).

Next, go through and make sure that you have page breaks in between each section. You want your chapters and title pages to start on individual pages. Also, make sure that after each title, you use no fewer than 2 lines to separate the title from the rest of the text.

Step 5: Almost ready to convert! Check your work.

QUICK & DIRTY TIP!

Make sure to hit "update" after each step. This ensures all changes are saved and ready to use.

Once you've gone through and made your changes to normalize and stylize the text, do a final pass to make sure that everything looks right. Sometimes in the process of formatting, things such as bold text, italics, and so on get lost. A quick run-through here can save you lots of headache later.

After you've ensured that your text is good, look at any pictures you may have embedded in your file. If you wish to insert any pictures, now would be the time to do this. Use the "insert" option at the top of the screen to add whatever picture file you'd like. Make sure that any picture you add into your manuscript has been compressed down and shrunk to at least 800x600. You can do this in Word, after you have inserted the picture. A picture menu will become available that will allow you to manipulate the picture you just inserted into the document. Reducing pictures will ensure that you don't weigh down the file and will help the picture to show up properly when it appears on the small screen.

Along with compression, make sure that your picture is set "in line with text," and that there is at least one hard return before and after it.

You do not need to convert the color to grayscale, as it will be automatically converted when read on the Kindle screen, but it will still show nicely in color for those who have the Kindle for PC application.

Step 6: Converting your Word document

MobiPocket Creator states it can use standard formats for conversion; however, I have found that saving your file as an HTML file is the easiest way to make it look like your original document. Trust me on this and save yourself the headache.

QUICK & DIRTY TIP!

There is a difference between saving as HTML/Web and "Filtered" HTMl/Web. You want Filtered.

Upload your HTML file into MobiPocket Creator, add your cover image, and convert.

Once you've uploaded your HTML file, you have a few more things to do. Add in your cover image, and then go to the TOC tab and set the first space to "h1." This tells the Creator to use those chapter titles you highlighted earlier as your Table of Contents.

Now you can convert it.

Step 7: Once you have uploaded and converted your file, you can upload it to the Amazon KDP page. Here you will be given a chance to preview your work before publishing.

If done correctly, you can have a clean-formatted Kindle-ready file in under two hours. As I said, it is a lot easier than the print formatting (though, after reading this, it might not seem so!).

QUICK & DIRTY TIP!

Download the Kindle for PC program. This is a free program that will read your PRC file. It's a good idea to check your work here before uploading it to KDP.

Kindle, however, isn't the only thing you have to format your book for. If you want it on the Nook, you'll still need to create an ePub file for Pubit! Check out Calibre for creating your ePub file. The process for using Calibre is very similar to the Kindle format. In fact, you may want to take your HTML formatted document—the one you used for uploading to MobiPocket—open it, and re-save it as a Word.doc with ePub as the extension. You will have a very easy time converting that through Calibre into your ePub-ready file.

Just remember that each time you save your file, give it a new name so you don't mix up your files.

Lastly, and probably the most tedious, to create is the Smashwords file. Because Smashwords will format your book for a wide variety of readers, it requires you to adhere to their specific formatting guidelines.

http://www.smashwords.com/b/52

I recommend you read through this guide very carefully before starting. Following their directions is key!

After all of that I hope I haven't scared you off ebook formatting. It can be a huge headache at times, but in the end, it's worth it.

Price

Now that you've gotten your book through the production phase, it's time to think about pricing. How much are you going to sell it for? What is too high? What is too low? What will earn the best profit and still attract readers?

With traditional publishing pushing ebooks into the higher prices and indie publishing pushing prices lower, there's a huge gap in the middle.

Amazon's pricing structure is set up so that anything $2.98 and lower earns a 35% royalty rate. Anything $2.99 up to $9.99 earns you a rate of 70% royalty. However, anything higher than $9.99 will reduce your rate back down to 35%.

So the sweet spot is that $2.99-$9.99 zone. That leaves a lot of space to work with and earn a very nice return on sales. But where do you price your book?

There is a huge debate going on in the indie circles today about pricing. What is fair? What is profitable? What's going to make you the most money? The two biggest price targets for debate are the $0.99 and the $2.99 price point.

That's a huge gap in prices, you may say. The reason for this gap is largely due to Amazon. At the lowest price point $0.99, you earn the minimum royalty of 35% on each sale. That means for every sale at this rate, you earn around $.35. That doesn't sound like much; however, sales in bulk will add up faster, and the lower price point attracts impulse buyers. This is the main reason you'll see a flood of books priced at this point. It's an entry-level price that is meant to attract new customers.

Now, this price point is also a good place for your shorter works: novellas, novelettes, and poetry collections. Anything that is not considered full-length is probably best priced at this level due to its shorter length. Customers tend to complain if they have to pay higher prices for something that can be read in an hour or less.

The $0.99 price point is also extremely attractive to impulse buyers. However, at that rate you have to sell thousands of books per month to really see any profit.

Amazon's system of pairing and advertising works to help promote books that are moving. You can use your sales ranking as a guide. Please note, the sales rank is not an official indicator of exact sales—it's just a gauge of how your book is doing in the market. The overall number is your rank among all books, and the corresponding categories below (if your rank is low enough) will indicate your spot in the various genres.

QUICK & DIRTY TIP!

If your book, priced at an impulse-buy level, gains enough traction in the market, it might get a bump in advertising from Amazon.

The drawback to the lower price is the general perception of lower price being equal to lower quality. Many people have a "you get what you pay for' attitude, and many more have been burned by the flood of new books on the market that should have been through more quality control before being published. Remember what I said about self-publishing being a dirty word? It still carries a bit of that stigma because many people are putting out work that needs more editing and maybe another round or two with a critique group. Sadly, the ease of publishing today and the stories of indies making millions push people to release work that is not yet ready.

So, in short, be careful with this price point. It is wonderful as an initial introduction to the market. It is great for your shorter works and as your loss leader for series novels, but it is not a standard you should use for all books.

At $2.99, the royalty payments are much higher. This is the magic number that raises you from a 35% cut of the profits to a whopping 70%. That means that for every sale at $2.99, you will earn roughly $2.00 (there are some other delivery charges involved at this price range here. Check the details of your Amazon agreement for exact numbers). As you can see, that's a pretty attractive number. And for most independent authors/publishers, this is the number I recommend using. You earn the most profit on your sales, while still remaining at a lower-tier price that is still attractive to readers.

$2.99 still carries a little stigma of "you get what you pay for," but it is not nearly as flooded as the $0.99 price point.

At this level, you will see a slowdown in sales. That same Amazon advertising structure that might have helped you at $0.99 will be harder to access at the higher price point, but it is not lost to you. Sales at this level are still somewhat impulse, but more often than not will be driven by your sample. All ebook retailers, Amazon being the biggest, offer sampling. This is like a reader in a bookstore picking up your book and reading the first chapter to see if they want to buy the book. No longer a pure impulse buy, people will download a sample and try it out before buying it. This is a double-edged sword. On the one hand, you want them to sample you and see if they really connect with your story. On the other hand, sampling takes away the impulse buy. People may download a sample and not get to it for weeks. With tons of cheap books out there, many people's reading lists are a mile long. That equates to slower sales initially.

On the positive, however, one sale at $2.99 equals six sales at 0.99 when you compare profits. So, even if sales are slower, the profits are much better.

As you continue to go up in price, you'll see the sales slow but the profits increase (as long as you stay under $9.99). The beauty of ebooks is the ability to play with your prices and find out the sweet spot for your particular book. In my experience it works as follows:

Novella: $0.99-$1.99

Novel: $2.99-$4.99

I would not suggest moving above the 4.99 price point unless you are selling an omnibus edition of your work.

Now, these prices I've been quoting are for fiction work. Non-fiction is a completely different beast. Self-help books and how-to books are the best sellers in this category, and they seem to start a higher price points.

Non-Fiction: $3.99-$6.99

Discounting & Price Matching

We talked a little about the three different channels to publish your ebook: Amazon, Pubit, and Smashwords. Of those three, two are standalone. Smashwords, however, is a multi-channel distributor. Smashwords will take your book and get it to Apple, Barnes & Noble, Sony, Kobo/Borders, the Diesel eBook Store with more channels opening all of the time. Through Smashwords you can make your book available as an app for the Apple iphone, Android, Windows Phone 7, and HP's WebOS. Having that large distribution network can be very beneficial. It can also pose some problems when it comes to pricing.

Companies like to offer the best price to their customers, and if one channel happens to discount your book, others will follow suit. Smashwords' distribution channel works off agency pricing, meaning the price you set is the price they sell for, no questions asked. However, due to the lag time in circulating updates to the network, price changes can cause a few hiccups.

Let's say you've had a book on sale for 0.99 for an entire month. You set the price on Pubit, Kindle, and Smashwords. The month ends, and you wish to raise your price back to the normal level. With Pubit and Kindle, you can have that change implemented in 24 hours. Smashwords may take a month or longer to filter that change through to all of its vendors. That means your book on Amazon, Barnes & Noble, and Smashwords main site might be at $2.99, and the other channels in the distribution network may not reflect that change immediately.

Kindle, for example, catches wind of these price differences very quickly and will mark your book down to match the lowest price available. If you price your books between 2.99 and 9.99 (opting for the 70% royalty option) and your book is on sale somewhere else, Amazon will discount to match the cheapest price available, and then pay you 70% on the discounted price. Please note: Don't abuse price matching. Competitive sites may remove your buy button if the competition goes on too long.

If you've priced your Kindle book at $2.98 or lower (opting for the 35% royalty option), you'll be paid on the retail price you set if your book gets discounted.

Here's one way to use this to your advantage. Amazon KDP does not allow indie authors/publishers to price books below $0.99, but some people want to offer a freebie every now and again. To force this, you can set your book to free via Smashwords and let Amazon price to match. You will not receive any royalty on your book, but it will be made available to the public as a free download on Kindle.

Marketing Basics

You've done everything and now have a book in your hot little hands, ready to sell.

Congratulations!

Wait, did you think you were finished?

No, no, this is just the beginning.

Now it's time to market it!

If you thought putting the book together was tough, you ain't seen nuthin yet!

That's the bottom line with self-publishing: You truly are alone in this. You are writer, publisher, and marketing executive all rolled into one.

Who are you going to get to buy your book? Friends and family will only take you so far, and many of them are more moral support than financial. Don't be surprised if only a select few members of your friends and family actually purchase your book. Hey, it happens.

What you need to do is get out there and pound the virtual pavement to push your book. If people don't know about your book, they certainly won't buy it. Promote, promote, promote.

Now, I did promise to give you the good, the bad, and the ugly. There is one thing you should know before we dive into marketing. Not every book is going to be a bestseller! Let's just rip that Band-Aid off right now. That means that no matter how much you throw into a book and its marketing, it may not make it big. Try your best and do everything you can, but don't sink all of your hopes into just one book. An author's career is based on all of their work, not just one title. So keep on writing while you work to promote your first book.

What's Your Platform?

"Platform" is a simple word to describe your presence in the marketplace. How do readers know you? How do they know your work? The answers to those questions are the building blocks of your platform.

The first step to finding and building your platform is defining your genre. Your genre will dictate your base audience. That lets you know who to target first with your marketing efforts. People who are avid Romance readers are different than those that are High Fantasy readers. Yes, people do read various genres; however, you want to make sure you are targeting the right group first. Work smarter, not harder.

Once you know who to connect with (genre-wise), you'll want to establish yourself. Platform is more than just genre. It's also perception. How will readers perceive you? What will they think when they hear your name? Are you a loudmouth cocky bastard who says whatever comes to mind? Or are you the soft-spoken wallflower who barely says a word?

Your personality and presence are part of the package. Your personality will have just as much effect on your platform as the genre you represent.

Think of radio personality Howard Stern. His personality is a very visible part of his platform. You may not listen to his show, but you know why you tune in or tune out based on his established personality.

Sometimes it is the interaction that people have with you that will drive them to your books.

Case in point: I am very active on Twitter, Facebook, and other various online channels. I love to chat with others, and through random chatting, not plugging my book, I gained a new reader.

One reader wrote this in her review of my debut novel,

Immortalis Carpe Noctem:

"Katie Salidas is, or I should say was, an unknown author to me. I have begun to follow numerous authors on twitter in the past months, but Ms. Salidas began to follow me first. I found her to be an excellent conversationalist, willing to chat at the drop of a, eh... tweet. She's known on twitter as @QuixoticKatie. The name alone intrigued and caused me to watch her stream and what she posts.

Generally, new authors email me or tweet me to request that I read and review their books. Ms. Salidas never did this. She has promoted her books herself and with the affection that she whips up in her following...."

If you'd like to read more of the review you can find it on Goodreads.com.

http://www.goodreads.com/book/show/7789362-immortalis-carpe-noctem#other_reviews

Platform is part genre, part finding your audience, and part personality (how you interact with them).

As an author, it's easy to want to hide behind your notebook and write, but as an indie author and publisher, you have a duty to market your books, and that means being social. You have to put yourself out there and be accessible to the public.

Create a strong and identifiable image of yourself and your book. Make your name synonymous with what you're promoting.

That is the basis of your platform and your starting point for marketing. Know your audience, know yourself, and be willing to get out there!

Putting Together a Press Kit

Once you know who you're targeting, you'll need to gather the tools necessary to market your work. A Press Kit is essential in the early stages. You will need:

An author photo

Your author picture is the only visual representation of you that readers see. Put your best face forward. The keg stand you did at your college party in 2000 might not be the best photo to use. You want something that is natural and shows you in your best light. Consider getting a few professional shots taken, or, if you're on a budget, have a friend follow you around with a camera and see what kind of candid shots you can come up with.

<u>Things to consider</u>

- Be current. Use a photo that's been taken within the last year or two at most. Outdated photos are not the most accurate representation of you.
- Be the focal point of the photo. It might seem cool to go with funky angles or wild backgrounds, but ultimately, you want your image to be the centerpiece of the picture. After all, it is your picture.
- Show your personality. Just because you're an author doesn't mean you have to show books in your picture. Your photo is a quick visual representation of you. What do you want people to see? Let your outfit, hair, and background all reflect you in some way.

An author bio

Your author bio gives people a little more information about you, the person behind the book. Make it cute and witty, but keep it short.

97

Always write your bio in the third person. But give it some personality. Think about who's going to be reading it. Who's your target audience? Make it entertaining for them.

Keep it short and sweet; under 250 words will do. No need for long-winded stories of your life.

If you have any noteworthy achievements, list them. If not, don't worry about it.

Relate your bio to your work. If you are a paranormal writer, think of how to link the paranormal your life. That may be as simple as stating what drew you to the genre.

Business cards

All professional people use business cards, and as an author, you are a writing professional. It goes without saying that you need one. These are an invaluable resource for promoting yourself and your work.

These little slips of paper are your calling card. You'll hand them out to everyone you meet, and through them, you'll build new contacts and draw potential readers.

Your business card should have:

- Name
- Title (use your genre here: Paranormal Romance Author)
- Web Address/Blog Address/Twitter address/Facebook address.
- Email address
- Phone Number (optional)
- Fax Number (optional)

Promo stuff (bookmarks, flyers, post cards, etc.)

Freebies and giveaways are a way to build good will and can potentially bring people back to your work. Bookmarks are especially handy for this as they are a multi-use item. But how do you create them, and how much is this "freebie" going to cost? That's a huge question.

As a self-published author, you learned the cost of putting together a book: the editing, cover design, and so on. Now, on top of all of that, you have to shell out more money to make things to give away, with no guarantee of return on investment?!

It might feel that way, but making these marketing tools don't have to be a big expense. You just have to find the right printer to do the work.

Bookmarks, while a free "giveaway," are not a pointless thing to sink money into. They are a multi-use marketing tool. A bookmark is something we all use. I have tons of bookmarks: some I love to collect and keep, and others are put to good use in many of my favorite books. By giving yours away to people, you are planting a seed. That person may not buy your book today, but they might use your bookmark when sitting down to read. Each time they use it, they see your book's image and your information. That can eventually lead to a sale.

Each bookmark you create should have two essential items on it: your book(s)' image(s) and a place where people can go to find you (Website or blog).

You can create your own images using photo editing software and then send them to the printer of your choice. Remember to do your homework and find the best price for your printing needs (because you are just going to give them all away. Don't break the bank on giveaways). The best bang for your buck I've found so far is **http://gotprint.net**.

I recently had a few new bookmarks created for my *Immortalis* series. For 1000 of each bookmark in full color (three separate bookmarks), I spent around $100. That breaks down to around 0.03 per bookmark. At that price, you can easily justify just giving them away! So, like I said, do your homework. You might find something even cheaper. Or, you can take my word for it and use **http://www.gotprint.net**.

A picture of your book cover

This is the digital age; you'll need some high-quality photos to email as well as ones to hand out to prospective readers! Make sure your photo is 300DPI (dots per inch) for anything that will be printed. For blogs and Websites, you may want to have a variety of smaller sizes available. It's always best to ask what size is needed before sending pictures off anywhere.

A summary sheet

A summary sheet consists of genre, publisher, publishing date, author, price, where to buy, and a short summary of the book. This is your handy dandy quick reference guide.

A media release (to announce your book)

There are a variety of outlets where you can send out notice of your new release. Having a media release prewritten and ready to go is always handy.

Approximately thirty copies of your book for giveaways

Thirty is always a good starting number; you'll probably give away more in your quest for reviews, but make sure you have at least thirty copies (print) to begin with.

These are your basic tools to begin your marketing quest.

Create a Marketing Plan

Now that you have the tools necessary to begin marketing your book, create a marketing plan. Set out basic guidelines for how you plan to reach your audience. (Note: you may not accomplish all of these tasks immediately. That's okay. Putting them down on paper helps ensure you don't forget them.) Here is an example of what your marketing plan should cover. We'll go into the specific "how to" details in later chapters.

Phase 1 – Internet –Social Network Marketing

Press Kit

- Set up an author press kit.
- Include links to any and all online author or book features such as blog interviews, guest spots, and book giveaways.

Create main Website, including:

- Author bio
- Multimedia content – book trailers, excerpts, images
- Sale of book in multiple media directly from Website ebook and print book
- Set up newsletter service and create signup link on main website

Blog tours

- Sign on with various review sites to gain honest reviews of book
- Seek out genre-specific blogs for guest appearances, interviews, and giveaways

Online Retail Sales
• Add Amazon blog and link to all testimonials link to main Website
• Add author info to Amazon profile page (Amazon Author Central: USA, UK, DE [Germany], & FR [France]. All separate sites for each Kindle outlet.)
• Add videos and any other media available to Amazon page
• Set up and promote sales through affiliate Amazon Store

Blog and social networking

• Drive traffic to main Website and encourage sales through blogging and social networking
• Link Facebook profile with other social networking sites
http://www.facebook.com
• Link Myspace profile with other social networking sites
http://www.myspace.com
• Link Goodreads profile with other social networking sites
http://www.goodreads.com
• Link Twitter profile with other social networking sites
http://twitter.com
• Check that LinkedIn profile has info on the book as well as the day job
http://www.linkedin.com
• Channel on YouTube for book-related videos
http://www.youtube.com/
• Create a profile on AuthorsDen.com
http://www.authorsden.com

Word of mouth and viral marketing

• Post videos on YouTube with excerpts from books

• Add signature file with book free offer and Website to all emails

Joint Ventures

Blog Cross-Promoting

• Invite other authors and business people to be guest bloggers or do interviews on your blog in exchange for space on their Website
• Participate in available blog hops and joint blogging events

Book Reviews

• Target genre-specific reviewers to solicit reviews

Phase 2 – Brick & Mortar Sales

Book Launch

• Approach local and independent bookstores to see if they will shelve your books or take books on consignment. (Every book store has a different person to contact. Go in person and talk to each store manager directly.)
• Donate books to your local library and offer to speak. (Check with local libraries first regarding their specific submission guidelines.)
• Inquire about local book fairs to participate in. The library is an excellent resource for this. Sell books at fairs.
• Launch at independent bookstores. Make sure local media is aware. Send a press release before and after.

Press Releases

• Send press releases for any and all newsworthy items relating to the book. Such releases will include events like author signings, new book format releases (hardcover, ebook, etc.).

Book Reviews

• Link online reviews from respected retailers and social "book review" sites.
• Use social networking sites such as Mysapce, Facebook, LinkedIn, etc., to spread the word about positive reviews.

Book Signings

• Target major retailers like Barnes & Noble and arrange for book signings at various locations locally.
• Target independent retailers and arrange for book signings.
• Be available for book signings in other cities around the United States.

Obtaining Book Reviews

Never, ever, ever, ever (I can't say this enough) ever pay for a book review.

For starters, they're never truly unbiased. If you're paying someone to review your book, there is an expectation of a great review on your part. No one wants to pay for a 1-star review, right? And if you take a look at the review-for-pay services out there, you'll notice a trend of nothing below 3 stars. Other people will notice this as well, and they won't trust what others say about how great your book is because you needed to pay for it.

So, how do you get your book reviewed?

Research blogs geared toward your genre.

This is an excellent place to start.
http://hampton-networks.com

Find out the review guidelines of each blog and shoot them an email politely requesting they consider reviewing your book. Be sure to include your:

Genre

Publishing date and publisher name (if it's you, say so. Be proud to be an indie!)

Word count

Synopsis

Whether there is any adult-related material in the book (some sites will not review anything with sex or foul language. Best to state it upfront.)

Format available (print or ebook)

Book cover image (People often judge a book by its cover, so let yours help sell it.)

You'll be surprised how many bloggers are out there, willing to look at your book. And it will only cost you at most the book plus shipping. At the least, it could be as cheap as emailing a PDF. Many of these bloggers don't just publish their reviews on their blog. Often, they also publish them on well-trafficked sites like Goodreads, Shelfari, Library Thing, and on occasion, right on your Amazon.com book page.

Shill Reviews

It's tempting to want to pad your books image with good reviews, but asking Mom and Dad (or any other family member) to post a five-star review will do more harm than good. The same applies to posting your own reviews.

Real readers can sniff out a fake review better than bloodhounds. That fake review might end up damaging you.

If you've followed the previous suggestion about locating book reviewers, you'll see there are hundreds of bloggers willing to read and provide reviews. A good quality book with an entertaining story is bound to get positive reviews. Be patient and look for real reviews; don't take the easy way out.

Along with obtaining legitimate reviews from bloggers, you may be tempted into review swaps with other authors. I would suggest not trapping yourself into this, but you may decide it is worth it.

A review swap is an exchange between you and another author. You both need reviews, and so you both agree to read and review each other's books. Sounds straightforward enough, but be warned this is a dangerous gray area and should be handled with care.

Not all self-published books are created equal. Not all authors take the time necessary to perfect their story. Not all authors could afford to hire out for editing. There are numerous ways that self-published books can differ in quality.

Eventually, you will run into a book that, for whatever reason, you just can't finish. The problem is, you've agreed to review this other author's work. If you review them honestly, they might sabotage your review. If you let it slide and "forget" to review their book, you'll never hear the end of it. After all, you did promise to review them. That leaves you with only one choice: to post a shill review.

This is why I say, tread carefully. Avoid putting yourself into this sticky situation at all cost. Again I refer back to the list above. There are hundreds of bloggers who will review your work, and there is no expectation of a return favor on your part. Stick with that method; it will serve you best.

Responding to Reviews

If at all possible, try to avoid reading reviews about your book. That will prevent you from being tempted to respond to them. However, we're all human, and we want to know when someone talks about our work. I can safely assume that you will ignore this advice completely.

So, once you've read a review on your work, you might be tempted to respond. The best advice I can give you for that is, no matter if they are good or bad, leave your book reviews alone.

Firstly, reviews are not written for you, the author. They are the reader's personal interpretation of your story. They need to feel free to share their thoughts, good or bad, without fear of harassment.

On bad reviews: Not everyone is going to like your book. A bad review does not mean the reviewer is personally attacking you. It's simply an opinion from one reader. You've heard the old saying about opinions, right? Everybody's got them...

It's human to feel upset when you receive a bad review. After all, you did labor over this project for countless months, revision upon revision. It's okay to be angry, hurt, disappointed, and any other negative emotion that hits you. Your work is your baby, and a bad review is akin to someone calling it ugly. As the author, you feel like any negative is a personal attack on you. Just feel it in the privacy of your own home. Remember, it's one opinion.

Lashing out publicly is never going to bring back positive results for you. In fact, it's going to push people further away from you and your books. Case in point: Recently, an author disagreed with a review posted by a blog <u>Big Al's Books and Pals</u> (dedicated to indie books). What started as a simple disagreement between the author and the reviewer's blog quickly dissolved into the author throwing a temper tantrum. This tantrum was tweeted, shared, linked and spread through the Internet like wildfire. The author's book took the brunt of the backlash and was flooded with thousands of negative comments and close to 100 1-star reviews.

The Internet is like an elephant: It never forgets. Any comments you make, whether bad or good, will be stored online, on servers, and can eventually be accessed and dragged out again when you least expect it.

Instead of channeling the negative energy into an online temper tantrum, which will only make you look bad, why not try to look for something you can take back from the review?

Did the reviewer point out any typos, spelling mistakes, grammar mistakes, etc.? Think of this as an opportunity to improve your work. The nice thing about being an indie author is we have the ability to update and improve our work. With ebooks, it's as simple as uploading a new file. The update costs us nothing and will correct the mistakes for any future books purchased. With POD books, the same principle applies (although due to cost, you might wait until you have significant improvements before uploading new files).

Blog Tours

Blog touring is an interesting concept. Instead of traveling the world for book signings with your print book, you can travel the blogosphere with your ebook. It gives you the potential to reach thousands upon thousands of people from the comfort of your own home.

This is something you can set up yourself, using the resource I mentioned above (ask a blog reviewer if they offer interviews or giveaways). It is a time-consuming process, though, arranging all of the tour dates, and you may not have the time available to set it up. If that be the case, you can have someone help you. That's where cost comes in.

Hiring a blog tour service can be extremely expensive or cost effective, depending on who you go with. The choice is yours. You have to factor in how much it will cost vs. how much interest it will gain for you and your book.

I've used a couple of tour services over the last year. My favorites include:

Virtual Book Tour Café
http://virtualbooktourcafe.weebly.com
Bewitching Book Tours
http://bewitchingbooktours.blogspot.com
The Bookish Snob Promotions
http://thebookishsnobtours.blogspot.com

Some things to consider when choosing a blog tour service:
• **What blogs are they affiliated with?**

Check out their links. They should provide a listing of blogs they regularly work with.

• **Do those blogs have a good following?**

Most blogs have a "followers" widget on the side where you can see how many people publically follow them. Also look at the comments section and see if people are participating in the blogger's posts. This will give you an idea of how active members are.

• Do they offer reviews with your tour?

Reviews are the biggest seller in these tours, because people trust their blogger's opinion. An interview is great to introduce yourself, but a "thumbs up" from a blogger who has read your book can help people decide to take a chance on you and your book.

• Does the blog tour offer giveaways for your book?

People like to win things. If your tour includes giveaways of your book or Amazon gift cards, etc., it will attract more attention.

Social Networking

Your online personality is part of your overall platform as an author. It's an excellent interactive experience for you and your readers.

However, you can't treat your online presence as a virtual billboard for your books. The biggest part of social networking is the *social* aspect. I'm sure you've heard this a million times, but you need to be active online. There is a caveat, though. "Active" means being a participant, not a spammer.

It's a good idea to have accounts at all of the standard social networking sites.

Facebook
Twitter
LinkedIn
Myspace

Beyond those, there are a few other book-related ones you should join as well.

Goodreads
Library Thing
Shelfari
Authors Den
Amazon Author Central

QUICK & DIRTY TIP!

Kindleboards is the single best resource I have found for indie authors. Just spend an hour combing through the Writers Café, and you will learn so much about writing, promoting, getting reviews, etc. I wish I had found this resource sooner.

Consider all of these as places to interact with your peers and readers. Notice I said "interact."

Remember, Don't Be A Spammer! It's okay to mention your books and the good things happening with them, but don't make that the only thing you talk about. No one wants to read a thousand lines of

"My book is out."

"I just released this book."

"I sold a copy of my new book."

"Did you know I have a new book out?"

"Have you bought my book yet?"

"Buy my book."

It gets old really quickly. Constantly marketing yourself and your work in your status updates will cause people to start clicking "unfriend" to shut you up. I was guilty of that in the beginning. And guess what, it didn't help my sales at all. In fact, I lost followers when I did that.

I'm not saying you can't mention your work, because you have to spread the word, but do it as part of your interaction with others, not as the intent of it.

If you're on Facebook, Myspace, LinkedIn, etc., before you even think to post something about your work, go through your friends list and make sure you have given other people's posts time and consideration. You're not the only one out there. Your followers are your audience and your potential readers. Keep them close. They are the ones who will (hopefully) buy your next book; you want them to know you care about them.

Social Networking Faux Pas

Here are a few quick social networking don'ts.

Don't directly ask someone to follow you.

There are millions of people online, and it may be tempting to contact them and suggest yourself as a person of interest. Trust me, don't do this. Instead of coming across as cool and interesting, you come across as the type of person who will spam their friends daily with request of "buy my book." Be interesting and social, toss out your screen name or Twitter handle when asked, but don't go begging for new followers.

Don't email or message strangers with advertisements for your book.

Don't contact random strangers or new followers and shove your book's information under their noses. If someone gets to know you, they will naturally learn about your book. That's a better sales pitch than the hard sell.

Don't use your social profile to only talk about yourself or your book.

Part of being social is the interacting. You are not interacting if you are just standing on your soap box screaming about your book.

Don't forget to proofread your posts.

You're an author—people will judge your spelling and grammar a little more harshly than they would any other average Joe's. Put your best face forward and quickly proof your post before you hit send.

Don't use links in every post.

If all you do online is post links, you will be ignored very quickly. This is not interacting with your audience. It's okay to post the occasional link, but your purpose for social networking is to be part of the conversation, not someone who stops the flow and directs traffic away.

Don't post hundreds of updates a day.

Posting too little can be troublesome, but posting too much is worse. Instead of being creative and witty, your posts become white noise among the throng of thousands of other people spamming the system. Only post when you have something worthwhile to say; otherwise, stick to commenting on your friends' posts.

Don't pester someone who stopped following you.

There are many social "helper" sites that will let you see who is and who is not following you. If someone has dropped you as a "friend," there was probably a good reason for it. Either you were not interacting with them, they did not like what you had to say, or you spammed them. No matter what the reason, leave them alone. Pestering a dropped follower is a sure-fire way to give you a bad reputation online!

Now that you know what you shouldn't do, here are a few things you want to make sure that you actually do.

Do join in the conversation.

Did one of the people you follow say something witty? Respond to it. Get in on any good conversations that are happening. That's the best way to be social and get to know your online friends.

Do share funny links, videos, posts, etc.

Just do it in moderation. Remember what I said above, don't spam the system.

Do ask questions in your post to promote social interaction.

I have found that asking the audience really gets people involved. I write about vampires and ask lots of opinions of my readers, wanting to know what they like and don't. The questions result in tons of responses.

QUICK & DIRTY TIP!

With Facebook, you have the ability to set up "Fan Pages." This can be a great way for you to make a separate space just for your author persona and books. This would be the best place to post your book-related news!

If you're on Twitter, scroll down through the tweets and get involved in the interesting conversations going on. Don't just sign on to post your latest update.

Twitter is an interesting site, which seems to have bred specific days where marketing and promoting are accepted. Take advantage of it. But again, *Don't be a spammer!*

#WW = Writer Wednesday. Don't post your link, but link to other great writers. They might link you back, and that helps you gain followers. Use #WW in front of a person's @ name to tweet about them.

Example: #WW @ihateuncleshady – awesome guy. Check out his work. (This is actually my hubby. He's not a writer, but he loves to post random craziness.)

#FF = Follow Friday. Similar to Writer Wednesday, this is where you can post links to your friends. Again, don't post yourself; this is to share the love. Often the people you link will link back to you, and this may help you gain followers.

Example: #FF @ihateuncleshady – awesome guy. Check out his work.

#samplesunday Post a link to a FREE sample of your current work.

Example: Read the first 2 chapters of Karma & Melodies #SampleSunday http://tinyurl.com/6bv9rhj

Remember not to be a spammer here. One or two posts spread throughout the day is okay. One post every ten minutes is BAD.

Also, while I'm on the subject of posting your promotions, remember that it's good manners to share the love. Do a bit of re-tweeting for your fellow authors too. Don't just make it all about you.

When I signed on to Twitter, I found an author group specifically geared to helping indie authors promote each other.

Independent Author Network

http://www.independentauthornetwork.com

Sign up here and be sure to help spread the word about your fellow indies. Don't just expect people to tweet about you. This is a collaborative effort.

Again though, I can't state it enough: Don't spend all day spamming Twitter about yourself or other authors. The occasional post every so often is good. But ultimately you need to be interacting, not advertising.

Social Oomph

It can be intimidating and overwhelming to think of all the Facebooking and Tweeting you might have to do to get your name and book out there. One utility I've found to be helpful with this is

http://www.socialoomph.com

This utility can help you track followers, set automatic updates, and much more. It's free for basic use and cheap for the "added features." Start with free, though, and see where that gets you.

The best use of this I've found is to automate your promotional post. I set up my weekly #WW, #FF, #SampleSunday, and book-related posts and then let the utility make the scheduled posts.

Again! Remember, do not be a spammer! (Are you sick of me saying that? Too bad. It's very important.)

Scheduling the promo stuff takes care of my marketing and leaves me free to interact with people while I'm actually there on the Website.

Make a Press Release

Traditionally published authors have the backup of a publishing house and a marketing team. One of the tools they use to help get the word out is a press release. It's effectively a nice, simple-to-read text advertisement that can be sent to news outlets to let them know about your book.

But you don't have to fret because you're an indie. There are ways for you to create and distribute a great press release too!

One of the places I use is PR Log
http://www.prlog.org

It's a free service that lets you create a nice looking press release that can be shared via a wide variety of social networks.

To make a nice, official press release, you'll want to do a few things:

1) Write a great eye-catching head line. This should include your title and genre.

2) Your first line should "announce" whatever you're promoting. Be sure to include: book title, release date, and author name.

*__Author__ releases the exciting sequel to **Book Name**, available at **Book Store** on **release date**.*

3) Include your jacket cover/synopsis.

4) Include an image of the book (if the news site allows it).

5) Include any quotes or review snippets you have for the book.

6) Include a listing of previous works.

7) Include contact info (email address) and links to purchase the book.

Websites & Blogging

An author needs a Web presence, a place where people can find you. A good author website includes a few key elements:

- **Photos!** Remember that author photo I recommend you take? Beyond your press kit, here's yet another place where you will use it. Along with your author photo, have photos of each of your books, upcoming and already released works.

- **Book information.** Your readers have probably stopped by your Website because they read your book or heard something about you. Now that you've got them on your site, give them all the information they desire. Just remember to keep it current.

- Your **contact information**. Sister Websites, social networking links, and email contact info is always handy to have. Don't make your readers search for it. Think of it this way: What if they are trying to send you fan mail? Make it easy and accessible.

- Along with your contact info, be sure to have your **bio** posted where people can easily find it. Readers want to know the author behind the book.

- **Book news**. Always be sure to post new content. Give readers a reason to keep coming back. This is also why a blog format website is great for authors. It makes it very easy for you to post new information.

- Lastly, be sure to have an **events schedule**. If you are planning any speaking engagements or book signings, make sure your readers know all about them.

Professional Websites can cost you a lot of money. Domain names need to be purchased, webhosting needs to be established, and for those of you who can't code a Website, you'll need a designer to make something that pops!

However, the costs associated with these things may not fit into the budget. If you can and want to afford it, great! More power to you. But, for those on a tighter budget, there are other ways of creating an online presence that won't break the bank. (And remember, you can always upgrade later as you become more successful.)

Most people will already have a blog via Blogger or Word-Press. Both of these are free to use, and you can add static pages for things like your author bio, book info, and books to purchase. With the purchase of your own domain name for around $10, you can even make the address something easy for readers to find, like:

www.yourname.com.

When I started, I wanted a professional-looking Website, but I also had limited funds. I compromised and paid for a Yahoo site and used one of their templates. It's not hideous, but it's not eye-catching either, and it doesn't get enough hits per month to make it worthwhile. That made me realize I didn't have to pay to have a Web presence. I already had a blog that gets a decent number of hits per day. Once my contract was up, I switched everything related to Rising Sign Books over to a new blog and took down the site I had been using.

Learn from my mistake. Rather than setting up a Website that carries costs like hosting, domain registering, and often needs site designing, why not create a free place on the web via Blogger? It costs nothing to set up a blog (no Web hosting fees required), they have templates available (no need to pay a designer), and it gives you a place to talk about your work.

Also, with Blogger's easy-to-use design templates and additional widgets, you can add things like PayPal buttons (to purchase print copies of your books), links to the various e-retailers carrying your book, or even reviews from sites like Goodreads.

Your Blogger post can also be configured to link to all of the other social networking sites such as:

Facebook
Twitter
Goodreads
Amazon Author Page
Myspace
LinkedIn

Book Signings

When I mention the words "book signing," you're probably thinking about that last book signing you attended for a big-name author. There were probably people lined up around the corner to see the author and get their books signed.

Sounds pretty exciting, right? I bet you're just imagining that happening to you someday. And maybe someday it will. Always keep a positive outlook.

However, for 95% of authors this isn't the case. Sorry, but it must be said.

That doesn't mean you need to get depressed and feel like your dreams of stardom have been dashed. It just means a slight reevaluation of the situation and a more realistic expectation of what will happen.

We indie authors have to work a bit harder for our fans. Let's face it, we have to work a bit harder for everything in this business. But we do it because we love it.

That doesn't mean that you can't still have a successful signing. Even if you don't think you have a single fan yet, you can still have a great book signing.

First things first. Change your idea of what a book signing is. Forget the screaming fans and lines out and around the bookstore. Let's be realistic here.

As an indie, a book signing is not a place for your adoring fans to come and find you. Sure, you might have a few friends stop by, your family might come to support you, but everyone else who stops by (for the most part) will be "new" to you.

Think of this as a way to create fans.

If you're at a bookstore, this is an opportunity to put your book in front of potential new readers. They are there looking for a new book to read. And guess what, you just happen to have a new book!

If you're attending a book fair, this is an opportunity to reach out to other booklovers. They are there because they love books.

And you are there because you love to write them. It's a match made in heaven.

If you're part of a "local authors" event put on by a library or any other book-related organization, this is an opportunity to reach out to your peers and maybe their readers as well. Everyone attending these events has a similar goal in mind to you, "sharing published work." Writers are also readers. Share, share, share.

Any of these events are places to build fans. If your book is available in print, you should be on the lookout for places to do book signings. Check with your local library, indie and big box book stores, and even smaller venues if you can find them. I once did a book signing at a neighborhood block party. It was out of the ordinary, sure, but I sold a few books. It was great.

So, once you've scheduled a book signing, what do you do next? How do you handle the event?

Let's start with the setup. You want your area to be perfect.

1) Have a nice presentation display. If you have a banner or framed book covers, even better. Make your table look nice and inviting. Bring a bowl of candy for people to munch on. Use a nice color-coordinated tablecloth to make your area stand out.

2) Have plenty of books on display. Bring more books than you need.

3) Have freebies like bookmarks, postcards, business cards, etc. People like free things, and if your book and information is on these free things, it will have more of an impact. People may not buy today, but they might use your bookmark and later decide to give you a try. With that said, make sure that your bookmarks and other freebies have something on them that tells where your book can be found.

4) Bring lots of markers and pens. You never want to be caught without a way to sign your book, right? Also, guard these like a hawk. I had all of my metallic sharpie markers stolen from my table when I walked away for a second to speak with the event coordinator. It's silly what people will steal these days.

5) Bring lots of water, but no snacks. Drinks are fine (non-alcoholic). You want to stay hydrated. But you don't want a

mouth full of crumbs when someone approaches your table to talk to you. Book signings are usually no more than a few hours. Eat before you get there and hold off on snacking until it's over.

Now we move on to the next part.

1) Look your best! Dress to impress. Go out and get your hair and nails done. Splurge on a mani/pedi. It will make you feel more confident, which will in turn make you look more approachable. Let's face it, when we look good we feel good. And you will want your spirits high when you go into that book signing.

2) Bring a wing-man (or woman). Bring a friend. Not only can they help you pass the time during a dry spell, but they can also help take pictures, watch the table during potty breaks, etc. A friend brings extra energy to a signing, and if you're anything like me (introvert is my middle name), they can also be your book's wing-man (or woman). Just like the wing-man at a bar, these friends can help talk up your book and make you seem like a superstar author. I can tell you all day long how great my book is, and you'll probably shrug it off. But, when another reader says it's great, you might stop and listen.

Okay, so you've got your table, you've dressed to impress, and you've brought your wingman; now what? Time to sign some books, right?

Now comes the hard part. Remember what I said above? This isn't going to be a line-out-the-door kind of event.

Now you have to work. Reach out and make some fans. The people passing by your table probably have no clue who you are. They might stop to take a second glance at your book. I'm sure you have a spectacular cover! So how do you approach them?

"Hey, buy my book!"

NO!

You may be ready to scream to the rafters about how awesome it is, but avoid the hard sell. No one likes it. It makes you seem like a used car salesman, and nobody likes them (my apologies to any used car salespeople out there).

Approach people in the same manner you would want to be approached. Do you want someone shoving a book in your hands and telling you to buy it? Probably not.

If they've stopped by, they might have an interest. So approach on that point. Greet them with a smile. Always smile. Ask them how they're doing. How's their day going? Ask them what genre they read. What was the last book they read? Who is their favorite author?

People love talking about themselves. Get them talking about the book-related subjects that interest them. They will hopefully warm up a little. Through chatting with people, you build rapport. You're no longer some random name on a book cover. You're a real person. Hey, maybe even a cool person.

At this point, you might be able to make a connection to their interest and your book. Ease into it; don't just shove it into their faces. Toss out some info on your book, how you were inspired to write it, etc.

A lot of advice on the Internet says, hand people a book to give them ownership of it. People are more willing to buy once it's in their hands. I say, take this advice with a grain of salt. Shoving a book in someone's hands makes me go back to the car salesman analogy. "C'mon, let's take her for a spin. You'll love it."

Tread carefully here. That's all I'm saying. You can certainly pick up a copy of your book and show it to them. But don't just shove it into their hands with the hopes they'll buy it. Remember you're trying to build a fan base here, as well as selling books. Offer it to them and see if they'll take it. If not, maybe suggest they take a bookmark or post card, something to remember you by.

Is every person who stops by your table a sale? Potentially, yes, but in reality, no. Many will chat with you, maybe take a bookmark or business card, maybe a piece of candy, and walk away. That's okay.

The point is you reached out to a person who didn't know who you were, and didn't know anything about your book. You've planted a seed that might eventually turn into a sale. Be sure to remind them, if they're walking away, that you're available on ebooks as well. I make it a point to always mention my Kindle, Nook, Sony, and Kobo availability at the end.

A successful signing is not always about selling hundreds of books, though that would be nice. It's considered a success if you sell as few as two books. That's right, I said two books.

The real success is in reaching people. Telling people you're out there. They may not buy today, but there is a chance, if you've made a connection, that they'll buy sometime down the road.

Book Trailers

Book trailers are a new trend in publishing. They're great for book promotion. But do you need one?

That question can really only be answered by you.

But rather than get into a debate on the need or lack thereof right now, let's talk a little about what they are and some of the ways they can be used.

In the past, all you had to promote your book was a cover and a quick blurb/synopsis. That old saying, "You can't judge a book by its cover," –that's a bunch of bull!

People can and will judge your book by the cover. You could have a stellar write up, and someone might still be turned off by the first image of it they see.

That's where a book trailer can help. Instead of having only a cover to present to people, you can also show them a visual representation of the blurb/summary. Much like a movie trailer, this can help to tease the reader and entice them to take a chance on your work. Please note, I said "can." There is no guarantee with book trailers.

Book trailers can be uploaded to a variety of places where people go to look for videos, YouTube being one of the most popular. This helps to give your trailer visibility. People love to watch online videos, right? With the right keywords, your trailer could become a viral video. Again... "could." There is no guarantee with book trailers.

They can also be used as part of your marketing plan. Are you going on blog tour? Include the embed code for each of your stops. This way you get maximum exposure while traveling the blogosphere. People love to watch videos, and they make a nice little way to finish up a guest post or interview.

Do you have a Website for yourself or your novels? This should go without saying but... make sure the video is there too!

Post it on your social networking profiles as well.

Facebook

Myspace

Goodreads

Amazon Author Central

Beyond that, there are also many sites dedicated to showcasing book trailers. If you have one, why not post it here?

Blazing Trailers

http://www.blazingtrailers.com

Book Trailer Matinee

http://www.facebook.com/pages/Book-Trailer-Matinee/128324860530296

Bookscreening

http://bookscreening.com

Preview the Book

http://www.previewthebook.com

Book Trailers

http://www.book-trailers.net

BookTrailers.ning

http://booktrailers.ning.com

Now with all that said, I am sure you're champing at the bit to get your book trailer made. But that brings us back to the original question: Do you really need one?

Book trailers sound like the perfect marketing tool. Who wouldn't want to have one, right? Well, there is a small catch.

If you can't make a book trailer yourself, this can be a costly "tool" to create. And (I've said it before... I'll say it again) there is no guarantee that you will get any sales from a book trailer. It's a tool. A very pretty tool, but it cannot make your book fly off of the shelves.

To make a book trailer, you'll need some royalty-free images, some royalty-free music, and a nice little program to tie it all together. You cannot use just any music or images as a book trailer is being used for commercial purposes. Creating a book trailer can be accomplished using Windows Movie Maker, iMovie (for Mac users), or an online site like One True Media.

For my first trailer, I attempted to go it alone.

It was a little more than a slide show, and some text with music. Not very flashy. Certainly not high-quality, but hey, it was relatively free, right?

Now, compare that to one that was professionally done... and you start to see why hiring out for this could be a better option. Let's face it, we're writers, but that doesn't mean we're all media artists.

Again I must state, there is no guarantee of added sales by having a book trailer. If you're thinking about hiring out for an artist to make your book trailer, you have to consider the cost. It's not going to be free. How much you want to dump into marketing? As I said before, these can be costly. I've seen book trailer creation sites out there with costs in the thousands and some with costs in the $10's. As with many things, you get what you pay for.

If you do want to go with something a little more polished and professional, consider these things:

Take a look at the previous trailers created by the site of your choice. Are they slide-show trailers? Are they animated? Are they actual movie clips? The level of complexity in the trailers will affect their overall cost. If your marketing funds are low, you might want to look at places that create simpler trailers. Even a slide-show, if done right, can look very nice.

Make sure that the person creating your trailer is really listening. Your trailer is a representation of your book. It needs to do a good job of that. And so does the person creating your trailer. Do they ask for summaries of your work to get a feel for the overall tone of the story? Do they make you an active part of locating the appropriate pictures? If your main character has blond hair, do you really want a brunette in your trailer? Communication with your artist is key.

Where do they get their photos? Pictures aren't free, and many of the ones found online require rights to be purchased to use. Most trailer creation sites will use royalty-free stock photos and music. The cost of those photos is usually factored into the cost of the trailer. It's always best to be sure you know where your photos come from.

Do they allow for revisions? Nothing ever comes out perfect the first time. Does your book trailer creator give you the option to make "reasonable" changes or alterations to the product before it is finalized?

Again, you can do this yourself. It's a time-consuming process that can be both frustrating and annoying. But, it can also be rewarding.

If, like me, you know your limitations but still desire to have this visual marketing tool, then do your homework and find a book trailer creator that is right for you.

The Importance of Tagging

What is a tag?

Well, when we are referring to our novels, a tag is a descriptive word or phrase that can help describe the book. This tag can refer to topic, genre, sub-genre, type of character, etc. Think of it as SEO (Search Engine Optimization) for your novel.

So what tags should we use?

Amazon.com allows each person to use up to 15 tags on any given product. Use every one of them for your book.

QUICK & DIRTY TIP!

Kindle books and print books count as separate products. If you have both, be sure to tag them separately. The same applies for the various outlets that sell your kindle book: Amazon UK, DE, & FR. Tag each book and version!

Here are the basics:

Book name – If people are looking for your book, they might just type that into the search bar. Having this as a tag means it should be the #1 thing to come up under this search.

Author name – Same reason as book name. Let's say they remember you wrote a book, but can't remember the title. If they search by your name, this will be one of the first things to come up.

Genre – People often search for things by genre. Paranormal romance, urban fantasy, modern gothic, etc. These are the search terms a reader might put in while looking for a book. Make sure you've covered all of your book's genres.

As a side note… On amazon.com, tags are associated not only with products but with discussion boards too. Appropriately tagging your book to the genre(s) it belongs to will also help link it to the right discussion board. Take a look at any book's product page, scroll all the way down, and you will see suggested discussions. This is more for you than for readers—it points you to the people you want to talk to. The people on these discussion boards are the potential audience for your book. Go say hi. But beware, Amazon forums are strict about advertising. *Don't do it* unless the forum specifically asks. Just go in, be friendly, and get to know the readers.

Theme – Are there any interesting themes to your book? Coping with depression, overcoming adversity, quitting smoking, fighting for survival, alien invasions. These can be keywords as well. Once you have the genre covered and your title and name tagged, move on to the themes that describe your book. Remember, you get 15 tags, so use every single one of them.

Creative but obscure references – Sometimes the genre tags and theme tags are so full of books or products associated with them that even if you had hundreds of votes, your book would not appear on the front. This is where creativity can come into play. Does your book have sex? Well, doesn't that take place in the bedroom (sometimes)? Did you know there are only 79 books tagged with "bed sheets"? If people are searching with that as a keyword, then your book stands a better chance of being seen among 79 than among the 6000+ books tagged with "urban fantasy." I'm not saying you should tag your book with "bed sheets" (unless you're writing erotica), but consider some of the more creative tags you could use.

Okay, So I Tagged My Book; Now What?

As I said before, tagging is kind of like SEO. It will help people find your books if they search. However, to make your book more visible, you have to make sure your book shows up at the top of the search.

Let's say I have my book *Hunters & Prey* tagged as urban fantasy. Well, currently, there are about 6,269 results that come up as urban fantasy. I need to get my book to show up within the first few pages for it to be effective.

The more votes you have on a specific tag, the higher it shows up in ranking on Amazon.com. So if you want your book and its tags to get recognition, you will have to do a few things.

Join a tagging community. No, not one of those street gangs out painting graffiti on the wall—a group of authors who help each other out by tagging each other's books. (This means you have to participate; don't just expect to get tags for nothing.)

http://tagmybookonamazon.wordpress.com
Tag My Book on Amazon (a great place to start your search for tag assistance).

Kindleboards – Join the community and visit the tagging thread in the Writer's Café.

http://www.facebook.com/pages/Amazon-Tags-Author-Assist/ Facebook Tagging group.

You can also ask your friends and family to help tag your books. It's as simple as logging into their Amazon account and clicking the check box next to the tags you've already set up.

So there you have it—tags are important for your book's visibility. Now go out and get your tags done.

Contests & Giveaways

One method to attract more readers is to host giveaways. You can offer a prize that will attract your audience in exchange for things like comments on your blog or tweeting about your book. These work well in conjunction with a blog tour. Word of mouth sells books! The more people there are talking about your book, the more chance people will buy it.

As an example:

On your blog, you post the release of your newest self-published book. You ask your friends and followers to share the info on the various social networks. For each mention on a different social network, they can earn one entry into the contest.

The prize, of course, should be something to motivate. Often just giving away a copy of your book is not motivational enough; however, a $25 gift card to Amazon.com might be.

Your followers should come back and tell you how many times they were able to share your book's information. Once the contest ends, add up each entry and draw a name at random to pick the winner.

That's not the only way to run a contest, but it is a simple example. Keep in mind, though, that prizes should not be too extravagant nor too cheap. You want something that will motivate people to talk about your work, but you don't want to break the bank trying to get new readers. Giving away something large like a Kindle or a Nook might not be the most cost-effective prize when you're starting out.

Giveaways

Giveaways are an excellent way to help gain readership and reviews. As mentioned before, when you are requesting book reviews, you are expected to give a copy away for free (either print or ebook).

There are other places to host giveaways that will give you some excellent exposure.

For print books, Goodreads is an excellent resource. If you have an account set up with them, click on your book's link and on the right-hand top corner (under Author Tools), you will see "List a giveaway."

This option lets you list your books via the Goodreads system. You can list as many copies as you want. You can make copies available to a variety of countries, or limit them to just the USA. You can also schedule how long that giveaway will be listed for.

Once you complete the setup for your giveaway, Goodreads takes it a step further and gives you widgets to advertise your giveaway on blogs and other social networking sites. These giveaways help get your book noticed. People like freebies!

Goodreads is not the only place to list your books for free. You can list them on your blog, or offer them to readers on your social networking sites.

Giveaways are a way to spread the word about your book without giving them all away. When people see things being given away too often, it can color their perception of the item. They may come to expect that it should always be free, or that it is not of good enough quality to be sold. Just remember, make your giveaways a special thing, not something that is offered every day.

Burnout

Burnout happens to us all. The constant drive to make time for marketing and make time for writing leaves you feeling stretched too far at both ends.

Being an indie author/publisher is a bit like being a jack-of-all-trades. You are responsible for every aspect of the product you create. That includes (as you have already learned) writing, editing, cover design, layout, pricing, and promoting. Even if you are contracting out part of the work to freelancers, you are still acting as overseer or project manager, and that's work too!

Indie publishing is a hard job, and often a thankless one. The only thanks you can hope to receive are spikes in sales or maybe a nice book review. Even then, the thanks is short-lived because you're constantly pushing for the next one and the one after that.

When you start out, you're a complete unknown. You have to really get out there and be with the readers. They have to get to know you and your work. The way to do that is to be in all of the places your readers might be. So, you set up profiles on Facebook, Twitter, LinkedIn, Goodreads, etc. Then, every day you religiously try to hit every single one and do your best to interact with the friends you've made. You post comments on their status updates, you respond to tweets, you participate in conversations on Goodreads about books in your favorite genre. As you do this, you learn about groups and message boards where authors are sharing good advice and working together to help promote each other's work. So you sign up for those too and add them to your daily round of "social networking." Some of the advice you get tells you that you must have a blog and use it regularly, so you create one and begin adding a daily post into your rotation. Soon you find that every waking moment is spent online and you have no more time for writing.

The upside is, you're beginning to see sales from all of your active networking. The readers you've been connecting with are really responding. Book reviews are coming in and you think you've finally hit it big.

Then, you relax a little on your daily regime. You miss a few blog posts, you forget to log into Twitter. A sudden downspike in sales happens and you are sure that it's because you haven't been online as much. Now you feel compelled to keep the same level of social activity because if you don't, your sales will suffer.

You immediately increase your networking efforts. Your fans begin to ask you about a sequel to your first book, but you just don't have the time to write it. You don't want to disappoint your fans, so you try to make time for it all and end up burning out.

Your story may not be exactly like the one I've just described, but I bet it has similar elements to it. You want to do everything you can to be online and be a good writer, but sometimes you have to draw the line.

It's hard figuring out the balance between the necessary social aspect of your job and the need to give your creative genius time to write. And I'm sure your family and friends would like to see you as well. I know mine do. They threaten to mutiny when I try to work weekends. And yes, it is "work," so don't be afraid to call it that. Indie publishing is a job!

What you need to do, when creating your marketing plan, is to work out a schedule that allows you time enough for everything without making you feel like you have to do it all every single day.

Blogging doesn't have to be an everyday job. And you're not going to lose fans if you aren't on Twitter or Facebook every second of the day.

Remember that utility I suggested you use in an earlier chapter? Social Oomph. Take advantage of its features and learn to schedule things like blog posts and Twitter updates in advance, so you give yourself more time for other things.

Along with scheduled updates, be sure to give yourself time limits on each site, so that you don't end up spending your entire afternoon online.

Make sure you schedule in writing time too.

Even with proper scheduling and limiting your time on the social stuff, you can still reach burnout. Know that it is okay to take a break from time to time. You do it in your normal job, right? Vacation, sick days, etc. Give yourself a break from marketing every now and again, so you don't end up burning yourself out so badly that you just can't stand to look at the computer. Trust me, your fans won't desert you.

Helpful Websites

Editing:

Sharazade's Editorial Service -
http://sharazade.fannypress.com/?p=825
A development editor and copy editor with over ten years of experience, including three years in-house with a New York publishing firm. Experienced with publishers and independent authors, fiction and non-fiction (including academic work).

Editing by Susan Helene Gottfried -
http://westofmars.com/west-of-mars/susans-editing-services/
With a BA in English Writing (journalism, PR, and fiction) from the University of Pittsburgh, and an MFA in Creative Writing (Fiction) from Bowling Green State University, Susan has the skills necessary to copy edit or proofread your work.

Red Adept Editing Service –
http://redadeptreviews.com/?page_id=4286
If you're an indie, you know about their book reviews. Recently, they decided to open up into editing too.

Autumn J. Conley –
http://www.facebook.com/pages/Autumn-J-Conley-Proofreader-and-Copy-Editor/133806322428
Proofreader & Copy Editor

Victory Editing -http://victoryediting.com/
A Variety of manuscript services including "Oops Detection" (final proofing).

Book Cover Creation:

Coverage – Book Covers (print and ebook) -
http://willsinrowe.blogspot.com
Professional book cover design at affordable prices!

Phatpuppy Art – **http://phatpuppyart.com**
Beautiful artwork available for purchase and use as book covers.

Printers

Lightning Source - **http://www.lightningsource.com**
Textstream - **http://www.baker-taylor.com/supplier_textstream_GetStarted.cfm**
GotPrint – **http://gotprint.net** Excellent printer for your bookmarks and flyers.

Royalty-Free Stock Photography

http://bigstockphoto.com
http://shutterstock.com
http://istockphoto.com
http://dreamstime.com
http://fotosearch.com
http://www.romancenovelcovers.com

Software & Tools

Self-Pub.net - **http://www.self-pub.net/wizard.html**
Provides software and services to help you get your book ready to be published. Their Book Design Wizard 2.0 is a very useful tool to help you properly format your print-ready book block. ***Not compatible with Mac computers**.

GIMP - **http://www.gimp.org**
This free image manipulation program will help you do the basic things you need to make a cover that can be used for ebooks.

Inkscape – **http://inkscape.org**

A free program that is similar to Adobe Illustrator.

MobiPocket Creator –
http://www.mobipocket.com/en/downloadsoft/productdetailscr eator.asp
This free program will help you format your manuscript for Kindle.
*Not compatible with Mac computers.

Calibre – **http://calibre-ebook.com**
Another free software utility that can help you format your books for ePub (Nook).
*Compatible with both PC and Mac computers.

Advertising

http://redadeptreviews.com Banner ads and sidebar book ads as cheap as $10
http://www.kindleboards.com Banner ads and Book of the Day ads $35-$195
http://kindlenationdaily.com Various ways to feature your work $89 -$299
http://www.projectwonderful.com Bid on various advertisements
http://thefrugalereader.com Various advertising packages
http://www.goodreads.com/advertisers Pay Per Click
http://ereadernewstoday.com/ Various advertising packages.

Legal Filings for your book

http://pcn.loc.gov To register for an LCCN or PCN, you will need to contact the Library of Congress.
www.myidentifiers.com Purchase your ISBNs.

http://www.copyright.gov File your US copyright online for as little as $35.00

MISC

http://www.critiquecircle.com Critique Circle is an online writer's workshop. It's members only, so any work you post for critique will not be searchable unless you are a member.
http://hampton-networks.com
An excellent listing of book review blogs.
http://www.socialoomph.com Social Oomph will help you to schedule and streamline your social networking updates.
Virtual Book Tour Café -
http://virtualbooktourcafe.weebly.com
Bewitching Book Tours -
http://bewitchingbooktours.blogspot.com
The Bookish Snob Promotions -
http://thebookishsnobtours.blogspot.com
Create free press releases with PRlog. **http://www.prlog.org**

Ebook Retailers

Barns & Noble PubIt! **http://pubit.barnesandnoble.com**
Amazon KDP **https://kdp.amazon.com**
Smashwords **http://www.smashwords.com**
All Romance Ebooks **http://www.allromanceebooks.com**
Book Strand **http://www.bookstrand.com**
Fictionwise **http://www.fictionwise.com**

Glossary of Publishing-related terms

Advance Review Copies (ARCs): Also known as galleys. These are prepublication editions of a book. They are generally used to generate reviews and publicity prior to the official release date.

Author: The creator or originator of any written work.

Alpha reader: The person or persons who are the first to read a completed manuscript. They offer feedback on the completed work as a whole, before it begins revisions.

Agent (literary/publishing): A professional representative of the author who, for a percentage of the profits, negotiates sales of rights for literary works.

Backmatter: Backmatter is additional information placed at the end of the book, such as: the appendix, bibliography, index, notes, and other references.

Beta reader: Like the alpha reader, this is a person or persons who read completed manuscripts and offers feedback. Unlike the alpha, a beta reader usually sees a manuscript after it has been through at least one revision.

Big 6: The six major New York publishers who dominate traditional publishing.

Blurbs (cover quotes): Endorsements of the book by well-known writers or celebrities. Often these appear on the book's front cover.

Book doctor: Someone hired by the author or publishing house to improve a manuscript. Often used interchangeably with editor in the freelance market.

Book blog tour: A relatively new method of marketing an author's book via online blogs. An author and their book will be scheduled at a variety of blogs for interviews, book features, guest posts, and chapter excerpts. This avoids the author needing to physically travel around the country, yet still gives them the opportunity to reach their audience.

Book trailer: A video "teaser" about the book. This can be in the form of an author interview or pictorial presentation of key plot points.

Blog: A blend of the terms Web and log. Blogs provide commentary or news on a particular subject, such as reviews on recently read books. Readers can interact with the owner of the blog via comments. This interactivity and "community" is an important aspect of blogging. It is also a useful tool for authors wanting to connect with readers. (See *Book Blog Tour*)

Critiquing partner/group: A person or a group of people who read and offer feedback and editing advice on some or all of an author's manuscript.

Copyright: The author's legal right to ownership of the work under federal copyright laws.

Cover art: The design of the book's outer image.

Cover quotes (blurbs): Celebrity or author endorsements placed on the front or back cover of a book.

Draft: The various pre-publication stages of a manuscript.

E-book/Ebook (electronic book): A book published in electronic form that can be downloaded to computers or handheld devices.

Editor: A person whose job is to locate and correct errors in a manuscript. There are various types of editors, each with unique functions.

   1. Substantive/developmental editor. This editor reads the book and tells the author what parts to tighten, what doesn't make sense, what plot threads need to be developed, etc.
   2. Line editor. This editor notes grammar issues, redundancies, punctuation issues, and awkward sentence structure.
   3. Copy editor. This editor intensively edits for continuity as well as grammar and spelling.
   4. Proofreader. This editor does a final read-through for obvious errors.

E-publisher: A publisher that focuses on publishing ebooks rather than printed books.

Fiction: A story invented by the author.

Freelance: Independent contractor hired to work in a variety of capacities on a book or article.

Galley: Bound edition of a work available for review and publicity purposes before publication.

Genre: Sales and marketing category into which the title falls (e.g. mystery, suspense, horror, how-to, self-help.)

Hardcover: A book with a hard cover.

Independent (indie) publishing/ Self-publishing: Often used synonymously, both terms refer to the process in which an author takes their manuscript from draft to printed book, incurring all cost involved in producing the work. Independent publishers *generally* take a more business-like approach, setting themselves up under a publishing name or label to produce multiple books, whereas self-publishers *generally* publishes under their own name and may or may not have multiple works to publish.

ISBN (International Standard Book Number): An ISBN is your publishing "social security number." It is a 13-digit string of numbers that identifies the book and publisher.

Manuscript (ms): The unedited book as written by the author.

Non-fiction: Written work that is factual.

Offset printing: A printing method used to produce large volumes of high-quality documents at a single time.

Paperback: A book with a soft paper cover

Print run: Number of copies produced at a single time (used with offset printing).

Print On Demand (POD): A printing technology and business process in which new copies of a book are not printed until an order has been received.

Proof copy: A draft of the book sent out for review before and approval production.

Publishing format: The physical form in which books appear—hardcover, mass market paperback, trade paperback, ebook, etc.

Royalties: A percentage of the sales price earned by the author on sold copies.

Synopsis: A 200-400 word summary of the entire book.

S.W.A.G.: Stuff We All Get. A common term at conferences and tradeshows describing the freebies that are given away. It is also used to describe the bookmarks, posters, and other book-related promotional items.

Traditional publishing: A process that involves several steps to entice someone else to take on the cost of publishing an author's manuscript. This involves but is not limited to: querying and signing with an agent, shopping a manuscript to editors, signing contracts, revising, and editing. In general, if successful, this process can take between 1-4 years from first draft to bookstore shelves.

Trade paperback: A paperback book that is generally 6x9 in size.

Vanity press (vanity publisher): A publisher who requires the author to pay for all of the publishing expenses. In return, the author receives a royalty on sales of each book.

Word count: The number of words in a work of fiction. They are broken down as follows:

> **Novel**: Generally, a work of fiction that is above 50,000 words. (Often the genre dictates what is considered novel-length. 50,000 is the bare minimum.)
> **Novella**: A work of fiction that is between 20,000 words and 50,000 words.
> **Novelette**: A work of fiction that is between 7,000 words and 20,000 words.
> **Short story**: A work of fiction that is under 7,000 words.
> **Flash fiction**: A work of fiction told in under 1,000 words.

Go Publish Yourself!

Index

Go Publish Yourself!

About the Author

Katie Salidas is a Super Woman! Endowed with special powers and abilities, beyond those of mortal women, she can get the munchkin off to gymnastics, cheerleading, Girl Scouts, and swim lessons. She can put hot food on the table while assisting with homework, baths, and bedtime... And, she still finds the time to keep the hubby happy (nudge nudge wink wink). She can do all of this and still have time to write.

And if you can believe all of those lies, there is some beautiful swamp land in Florida for sale...

Katie Salidas resides in Las Vegas, Nevada. Mother, wife, and author, she does try to do it all, often causing sleep deprivation and many nights passed out at the computer. Writing books is her passion, and she hopes that her passion will bring you hours of entertainment.

http://www.katiesalidas.com
Facebook
http://www.facebook.com/pages/Katie-Salidas-Author
Twitter
http://twitter.com/QuixoticKatie

Other Books by Katie Salidas

Immortalis Carpe Noctem (Book 1)

Becoming a vampire is easy. Living with the condition... that's the hard part.

Bleeding to death after brutal mugging, twenty-five year old Alyssa is rescued by the most unlikely hero: the handsome and aloof vampire, Lysander. His gift of immortal blood initiates Alyssa into a frightening, eternally dark world filled with: blood-lust, religious fanaticism, and thousand-year old vendettas.

With Lysander as her guide, Alyssa will have to learn what it takes to survive in the immortal world. She'll have to find the strength to accept her new reality and carpe noctem; or give in and submit to final death.

Hunters & Prey (Book 2)

Becoming a vampire saved Alyssa from death, but the price was high: the loss of everything and everyone attached to her mortal life. She's still learning to cope when a surprise confrontation with Santino Vitale, the Acta Sanctorum's most fearsome hunter, sends her fleeing back to the world she once knew, and Fallon, the friend she's missed more than anything.

Alyssa breaks vampire law by revealing her new true self to her old friend, a fact which causes strong division in the group that should support her most: her clan.

Pandora's Box (Book 3)

After a few months as a vampire, Alyssa thought she'd learned all she needed to know about the supernatural world. But her confidence is shattered by the delivery of a mysterious package – a Pandora's Box.

Seemingly innocuous, the box is in reality an ancient prison, generated by a magic more powerful than anyone in her clan has ever known. But what manner of evil could need such force to contain it?

When the box is opened, the sinister creature within is released, and only supernatural blood will satiate its thirst. The clan soon learns how it feels when the hunter becomes the hunted.

Apparently powerless against the ancient evil, the clan flees Las Vegas for Boston, with only a slim hope for salvation. Could Lysander's old journals hold the key? And what if they don't?

And how welcome will they be in a city run by a whole different kind of supernatural being?

Werewolves…

To purchase the *Immortalis* books (in print and ebook):

Amazon USA
http://www.amazon.com/Katie-Salidas/e/B003APXXWO/ref=ntt_athr_dp_pel_1

Amazon UK
http://www.amazon.co.uk/Katie-Salidas/e/B003APXXWO/ref=ntt_athr_dp_pel_pop_1

Amazon DE (Germany)
http://www.amazon.co.de/Katie-Salidas/e/B003APXXWO/ref=ntt_athr_dp_pel_pop_1

Barnes & Noble
http://productsearch.barnesandnoble.com/search/results.aspx?WRD=katie+salidas&page=index&prod=univ&choice=allproducts&query=katie+salidas&flag=False&pos=-1&box=katie+salida&ugrp=2

Smashwords
http://www.smashwords.com/profile/view/KatieSalidas

CPSIA information can be obtained at www.ICGtesting.com
Printed in the USA
BVOW060419280312

286247BV00001B/2/P